Growth Manifesto

-Self Conscious Liberation-

Talonie Starr

Acknowledgements

First, I would like to thank God for everything. I thank You for allowing me to see a glimpse of you through my hardships and my triumphs. I thank You for giving me a mind to understand the fragmented parts of You and still stand in amazement. I thank You for my big brother Jesus, who set the example for me, to be real and naked at all cost. I can't forget the Holy Ghost, which served as a companion wooing my sanity to stay with my person.

I thank you my best friend. You are beyond words. I just hope that I get the opportunity in this life to serve you as diligently as you have me. Thank you for your patience and kindness. I thank you my mirror. What can I say to you that you don't already know? Thank you for my reflection of truth.

I thank you my sisters who have prayed for me when nothing else worked. Thank you for showing your love, your frailty and your beauty. I thank you my brothers for all the wacky demonstrations of masculinity. Thank you for your sit down, and your stand up moments.

I thank you my mother. You are so beautiful to me. You who conceived me in thought first. Thank you. Thank you for your spirit. You have the passion of a Phoenix. I cherish every experience and I hold dear every lesson. I thank you for the fires in you belly that forces light out of darkness.

I thank you my father. You are my mystic dreamer. You who went to places well unknown and came back to make me host questions. Thank you for the seeds of wonderment. Thank you for the drive to keep going. You are and forever will be my lion.

I thank those that I have not met, but have touched me through their journeys. I thank you Oprah for giving me something to see past my socio-economic status. I thank you India.Arie for giving me beauty to sing about. I thank you Tyra for that show about eating disorders. It sparked me to tell my story. I thank you Barbara Jordan, Flo Jo, Queen Namina, Maya Angelo, and so many others who have contributed to the development of my search. I thank you Socrates, Descartes, Plato, Malcolm and Martin, and N. Walsch for thinking bigger. I thank you Martin Luther, for being not controversial, but consumed with the will of the people. Thank you.

FOREWORD

Hey Girl,

I like the book and I like your style. ... I've always
known you were talented. This is no surprise to me. We
share the same blood and DNA. Greatness runs through
your veins and wisdom flows from your words. Yes, you
are ahead of your time and your experiences. But that's
what I like about you. Yes you. You are special. Special
people like yourself are to be shaped, molded, and set on
fire so your life will be a flame to those whose light has
gone out. Be the light. Yes, be the light and set others
free.... You are too deep for me. However, I am
learning a lot from you and my professors.
Everyone has an interpretation or meaning about words.
Again, the language in your book does not offend me
and I believe you are going to help a lot of people.
Every generation has a common way of communication
with one another. You will reach the audience you want
to help. Continue to help those who need you and
continue to be the person you are. Daddy would be so
proud of you. If he were alive, he would probably
demonstrate how you could use profanity with power
while you are performing on stage. Better yet, he would
try to get on stage and actually try to coach you and
create a scene where someone is acting out your words.

Anyways, as I always said, be an Original, Not a Copy!

It is time to go into print. And yes, the poetry section
under African American section will be just fine.

Love,

Ronnie

Warning!

This book contains material that my not be suitable for certain audiences. All experiences represented are real, but only holds one perception of observation. All names have been changed to protect the innocent. Viewer discretion is advised.

ISBN: 978-0-6151-4141-1

Table of Contents

Introduction

I am thinking if I should even tell you about the things in this book. I want to somehow prepare you for the content. I wish to explain my rational as to why it exists. My simple answer to that is this, plainly: I wrote down those things that most individuals, in a church setting refuse to talk about. I know. How can I generalize so easily? How can I give information on issues for which I did not receive a doctorate or an ordainment? I don't know. I never claim to have all the answers. I do know that there are people out there who need me. There are people out there who want to give up. These individuals have everyday occurrences that chip away the beauty of their existence. So I write.

I find it difficult to understand how there are so many righteous people, all over the world, proclaiming different teachings, who refuse to get their hands dirty. I don't understand how language and lifestyle easily offend those that are supposed to defend? In this work, you will find the dirt of me. I will give you a fragmented picture of pews not sat in, pulpits covered with scorpions, and love lost in the movement of wind. I critique myself as a righteous person. My observation is displayed through poems, journal entries, essays, prayers, and performance. I wish to understand the balance that is my human frailty and the entity that I call the soul. I encourage you to chew through this, not just for yourself, but also for that person who sits next to you on the train. I hope that you read and ask yourself mighty questions that may change the way you thought the world to be. I challenge you to be a door that someone uses to find peace and tranquility.

In The Beginning...

From the mouths of babes…

My Story

Life; what a beautiful story. Some people might have the strength to argue with it because this statement is false to them. But with me, life has its ups and downs. Sometimes the bad outweighs the good but in the end, victory reins with things of prosperity. My story starts off on August 8th, 1979. Born to Sarah and Abraham is a healthy baby girl! Goodness this child is eight pounds and four ounces. This is where it begins. The small pebble of snow that is at the top of the mountain that was just blown down from the wind. My recent, or more so earliest memories are about my parents. I don't know the place or the time. As a child I found myself crying, not because of the fact that I was a child, but because I was hurt. I was walking down a big hallway. Someone was screaming. There in the faint light was Deddy hurting Ma. She told me to go get help. What am I to do? I yelled for my brothers but no one listened or heard. Mama got up and ran to the kitchen. All the kids behind her are trying to see what was going on. Especially me. "Ma why do you have that knife!" No one could hear me. I was too small. That night was a total blur. My three brothers and I were all moved around with relatives. "Now you know that people are going to talk, so let um." Grandma said. Mama and Deddy decided that they were leaving each other.

Mama had those friends. She called them her sisters. My folks were always in the entertainment business, you know, strippers. They were strippers since I can remember. Many nights they would bring me back candy. Often they would tuck me in. I would wait a while and I would go down stairs to see what they were doing. There would be a whole lot of money on the table. So whatever they did, they did it well. Oh yeah, I was telling you about these sisters. It was a lot of them. Mama would go over their house and they would have a hen party. Saying stuff like "Hey girl, can you believe so and so." It would go on all night. They would talk and talk. Almost like forever. Mama had a baby by this time. It was a boy. We are going to call him Brat. Anyway, one of my mother's sisters had four kids, three boys and one girl. I used to go over there because they would baby-sit me. Three of them were older than me. They were about eight to twelve years older. Later on, they started being a little too friendly. They touched, poked, licked, and grabbed places I never knew existed. Many times I got sick because I did not like it. I cried. I bled. I left. I was about five, so I could not go anywhere. When I state that I left, I mean spiritually…. My body was going through so much hell that my soul could not take it. At first they would hit me because I would not cooperate, but when you are just going to die you don't care anymore. It later became routine. A child should not ever have to go through what I've been through but many children do. I was just blessed that it ended. I stayed in that situation for about a year. My baby brother was walking then. The physical abuse stopped but not the mental abuse. These teenagers scolded me, laughed at me, picked at me until I could not take it anymore. So around Christmas, I finally told someone. My brother that is eight years older than me was there, my Mama and Brat. I said that they hurt me. Now I don't know what happened after that. Maybe they heard me and hurt them or maybe they didn't hear me at all.

It got real hard when my parents split up. Mama had all the kids. I can remember one of my older brothers feeding me army rations. We had to do what we had to do in order to survive. I was not in school at that time. That was good to a point because

Ma did not want people to see her little princess in poverty. I started school anyway because it was against the law not to. Those teens that I told you about never touched me again, but I did see most of them throughout my life.

Deddy had it hard too. I never knew what he did in order to survive, but he did it. Deddy and Ma had their differences, but they were real parents. Even though they were apart, they still managed to keep the family together. Later, while I was in grammar school, I stayed with Deddy for a while. My brother, who was eight years older than I, was also there. We took good care of each other. Those times were terrible. We lived in an abandoned house. It was not always abandoned because the whole family used to lived there. But the bills where so high and you can figure out the rest. Anyway, when it got cold, Deddy put the hot plate in one room. This is where we three stayed. We ate, slept and had our talks there. In spite of hard times there were good times. Deddy would ask how our day went and how we were. Now I know you are asking yourself how did we eat? Well here's how. My brother would save his lunch from high school and Deddy would work at Manpower. So we ate. Prior to that, our neighbors were good friends of ours and they helped too. See, the way the houses were is interesting. Their house was in front of ours, you could walk out our front door and you would be at their back door. This was within two yards. I stayed with Deddy until the school year was over; prior to that I stayed with Ma.

Ma was still an entertainer, so she had entertainers as friends. All my brothers were there and so were other people. Some I knew, and some I didn't. They all lived there. The place was big. It was a 2-flat on the southeast side. We all lived upstairs. It had two bathrooms, five bedrooms, living and dining rooms and a kitchen. I did not like it there. It was too spooky. Crazy things happened. I can only share a few.

I had a beautiful porcelain tiger. I loved it because it was big and I would talk to it and it to me. She said that she would protect me. I feel to this day that she did. One day, some people were arguing and the big mirror came down and sliced her head off. It was such a clean cut that you thought that she was made of flesh. I was hurt. I knew that evil had done it and I did not want it to happen to me.

After that, I was a wreck, but I was stable. I was stable because I used to go over my Aunt Pea's house. She would press and comb my beautiful long brown hair. My hair was so pretty. She taught me about being a queen. She also taught me about Christianity. She taught me to love the Lord and how he would love me.

Soon, I had to return home.

It was hot. My brothers were clowning. They were teens. They would have girls over and do all sorts of stuff while the grownups were gone. One time, one of their friends drank a cup of water with a roach in it. He was drunk. Well, it was summer and I could not stay in the house forever, so I went out. I met this girl named Holly. She was cool. She was a tomboy like myself. She was my friend.

Holly and I were like twin sisters. When she went somewhere I was there. When I went somewhere she was there. Holly taught me stuff. Holly was abused so she shared her tears with mine. Even though we were bullies, we were harmless flowers. I loved her so much because she loved me. We cried together, and prayed together. That was my true best friend.

Another one of these creepy times was when my brothers were having a coed sleepover. Our parents knew all of them so I guess it was all right. While I was sleeping, *I dreamt that I was in the house where I was. I could see everyone sleeping but there was someone in the corner. He was dressed in all black with a black top hat. He was reaching for me and I began screaming. But no one heard me. So I screamed louder and louder but all I could hear was silence.* All of a sudden everyone was looking at me when they woke me up. They said I was screaming. Now that is mighty strange when something like that happens. I told everyone that evil was in there but they didn't believe me. After that a whole lot of stuff happened. A car hit one of my older brothers. Another on of my brothers was diagnosed mentally handicapped. Sex, crime, and violence fell on the house. I began playing with knives and etc. Finally, after some time, we moved.

Yeah, we moved, but right down the street. This time Mama didn't let everyone come along. My brothers were bad teenagers -or at least their friends were. I can remember guys around a round table. It had dead, crumbled leaves on it. I know now that these leaves were marijuana. The aroma would be thick. I think I got a buzz from smelling it because I thought that a white pick shouldn't make a shadow on a white wall. I don't remember that place too much; I don't think we stayed there that long.

It is kind of hard, trying to recall everything. Some things are just not meant to be brought back up. I relate the date with my schooling. Even though I moved around I was still in school. So when a memory comes, I think of what school I was attending.

My family started going to church. We were new members and we found the experience to be very interesting. My mother felt the spirit as she walked in. I was there because there was this cute boy. Even though I was young, I knew all about body parts and sex and stuff, because I used to watch freaky shows on TV. Anyway, this boy was so cute; the only problem was that he only came, like, every blue moon. He was a short, round; cocoa-skinned young man who was a year older than me. I was fascinated with him but he didn't go for my type. I was tall for my age. I had short hair, from a botched Jerry Curl, and I was kind of dark. He liked the longhaired, short, light skinned girls. So in order for me to get this mini He-man, I had to use my wits and my words. His parents were beautiful people. His father was a preacher. My mother's friend introduced his parents to mine and we later attended his parents' church.

The Teenage Psyche

Use words when necessary.

My Broken Heart

During people's lives they come to a point where expectations turn into disasters. I can truly say trying to date a supposed friend can be difficult. The situation is this: I was interested in this guy. We were real close. I would speak to him in a flirtatious manner and he would respond with pleasure and delight. I was attracted and I wanted this individual. I felt that he was worth the time and effort because I knew him, or, I felt I did. Later, we spent some time together. It was on the personal tip, so I thought. We really had a chance to become more than friends. We returned to our place of enlightenment and the situation had totally changed. The feelings that I felt were not mutual. It crushed me. I did not cry outside, but inside, I was weeping. I feel that if you don't plan on being with someone tell him or her in the beginning, so no one's heart will be broken.

Diagnosis: Unwanted Love

If I won the lottery

Gambling is a sin, but if I won the lottery, I would give half of it away. I would do this because a number of people have inspired me and helped me. Money does not mean that much to me because I feel that if you have things like friends, love, God, family, you don't need money to make you happy. Don't get me wrong, I do enjoy spending money, but I will not let it control or change my personality.

Diagnosis: Comments from the Church

If I were a piece of clothing...

... This is what I would be. I would be a jacket. It does not make a difference what type of jacket. I chose a jacket because I would be used to keep you warm when you are chilled. I will hold and comfort you with security. I will not just be used for warmth. I will also be a shield to protect your inner wear. I like the jacket because I will always be seen and noticed.

Diagnosis: Addiction to Attention

What inspires me?

Inspiration is a beautiful thing. It is so wonderful because artists use it in order too paint, sing, act, dance, etc. The colors and contrast [of pictures] are all inspired by something. Inspiration can dwell in anything and everything. A lot of things inspire me. My friends are my inspiration. When I see a sunrise and a sunset I am inspired, and when I am in a large building with creative architectural designs, it inspires me to sing, dance, or just to stay positive and happy.

Diagnosis: Birth of an Artist

How does God fit in my life?

A number of individuals have religion in their lives. This is there to make a person more aware of their spiritually. It also keeps you physically and mentally balanced. I strongly believe in this. As a matter of fact, I participate in such a belief. My religion is Christianity. I believe in the Holy Trinity.

This consists of the Father, Son and Holy Spirit. I attend church service regularly and I enjoy doing this. I am Christian because I feel that that is the best decision that I have ever made. It has made me very mature with life and my surroundings.

Diagnosis: Declaration of Independence

If the World was filled with all teenagers...

... I think that the world would be the same. This is because teens act or sometimes try to act as adults. Our parents would be more understanding, and so would our teachers because they would be the same age. I don't think there would be any wars because people would fist fight or play video games to solve the situation. It would be a lot more freedom because there won't be a curfew or regulations. It would be productive.

Diagnosis: Theory of Relativity

One possession I will have in my last will and testament, who I will leave it to and why would I leave it to that person...

Have you ever had something that you treasured? Maybe it was just a family heirloom passed down. Regardless about how you got it, the point is that you have it. I am one of those many people who have such darling pleasures. The processions that I have are my mother's wedding rings. They are white gold and the engagement band has a small diamond in the middle. The way that the rings are designed makes it special in itself. I will leave this to my first-born daughter as a sweet sixteen-birthday present because this is when my mother gave it to me. Hopefully, I will be living at that time.

Diagnosis: A Mother is God in the eyes of a Child

Is parting from a friend such sweet sorrow?

Throughout our lives we have friends. Sometimes there is a time where we have to separate from this special person. Most of these separations are caused because one party has moved away from another party. Mine is just a little different. I have a number of male friends. They are very special to me and I appreciate their time in being a friend. The only problem is that I would either become attracted to them or they to me. In this attraction, the friendship no longer is a friendship. Sometimes a relationship began but mostly all of the time one ends up being hurt. So in this situation I find myself parting from this friend. So I can honestly say in some situations that parting from a friend can become sweet sorrow.

Diagnosis: Root of Rejection

My love for you

Dear You,

My love for you is hard to explain. I was not the same person after you came. The way you are is so unique. You sometimes tend to be discrete. We met on a day of grace and bliss. You changed my life with a gentle kiss. When I see you I feel so alive. The thoughts of happiness I can't describe. I am blessed that I found someone like you. I am happy that your love is true. We have our set backs and we have our downs. Then the tides of happiness turn it all around. You leave me speechless when you hold me tight. You ease my pain and make problems right. This is the reason for my love for you. I love you because of the things you do. I love you because you always speak your mind. Sometimes you are speechless, but the words you will find.

Love,
Pleased

PS. Thank you for making my life a new. Thank you for my love for you.

Diagnosis: Very first Luther Song

My First Love

My first love was my friend. As a matter of fact, he was my best friend. When I first saw him I did not like him. He was a pimple-faced teenager. I knew him for a long time. I met him at 11 years old; I began dating him at 12. My parents would not ever approve, so everything had to be kept quite. He would call me and talk to me on the phone. He would call to see how I was, and if there was anything that he could do. I began loving him at 14. Age doesn't matter at all. We would talk, and when we got older we took walks on the beach at sunset. He would hold me and tell me that everything was all right. He would wipe my tears and hold me when I was cold. When I was working, he would come to my mom's apartment and clean up. He never argued with me or at me. He was serious and silly. He kind of reminds you of Shaun and Marlon

Wayans, but put together. You can tell when you love someone: it shows when the infatuation is over. You love the person's faults and their good deeds. You claim them when they fall and you help them get back on their feet. Love was real with him and I. We went our separate ways because we were getting too deeply involved. So we didn't break up on bad terms. We are still close to this day. He is my best friend and I am his. I do love him as he loves me. As time progress he may be my final love and only love.

Diagnosis: Boy Next Door Syndrome

Time Travel

I designed a time travel unit, which allowed me to see my life in 20 years. Here in 1996, I was placed in 2016. My trip was very smooth. I arrived in my back yard or I think that is what it was. It was huge. The yard stretched as far as the eye can see. There before me was an 18th century mansion. As I walked toward the front of the estate it was so beautiful. Everything was very glamorous, but historical. The large fountain was very beautiful in the night air. As you walked to the door, one was greeted by the trail light. It said welcome to the estate of (fill in the blank). I walked in. There were two stairways that led to the second floor. They were in a swivel motion. Each room had a theme to it. There was a 1920's room, computer room, nursery, toy room and my favorite room was the studio. It did not look like a regular studio. It was all shades of blue. It had a wall where it would open to the outside. The floor rotated. You could speak to the main computer and it would change the surroundings for a different inspiration. That is where I saw myself. I was trapped in a form fitted purple dress. It covered everything from my neck to my ankles, but it was a little revealing. I am gorgeous. I said that I was expecting me. She showed me my children. I had two sets of twins and one girl. Our husband was fine. I asked myself how did we get this. I said, "in time I will know."

Diagnosis: Attention to Self

The fight I never forgot

During people's lives they have conflicts. Some of these disputes are physical. You can go around and ask a person about a fight and they will explain or describe confrontations where one person hits or beats another person. My fight was different. It was difficult to win but in the long run, I won. My battle was reading.

As a young child, I was considered gifted. I had special abilities that made me dominant in many areas, but fragile in academics. My family had traveled around a lot so this made my reading terrible. I could recite my alphabet, but actual reading in front of the class was challenging. I made it seem like I was shy, but that did not last very long. Finally, my teacher noticed that I had a problem, so she helped. We read before school, after, and at recess, and at lunchtime. I mean, all the time. I still have the book we practiced out of. I won this battle because I can read proficiently, and I can help the other 3rd grade Talonie's out there.

Diagnosis: Awakening of a Revolutionary

OUT BURST

HAPPY COMFORT DAY FOR TWO.
BRINGS ME TO THIS RELAXED POINT OF VIEW.
I SIT ON MY COUCH AND WONDER.
ABOUT THOSE PLACES FAR FROM YONDER.
IS IT POSSIBLE THAT MY MINDS AT DRIFTS?
NEEDING A BOOST OR A HELPFUL LIFT.
I SIT AND SEE MYSELF IN THE PAST.
THINKING OF THOSE DAYS THAT WERE FAST.
THINKING OF THE DAYS LONG AGO.
THINKING OF HOW HE LOVED ME SO.
MANY SAID THAT IT WOULD FAIL TO GIVE,
BUT IN THOSE DAYS I CHOSE TO LIVE.
I SIT AND CRY ALL MY NIGHTS,
HOPING THAT MY LIFE WOULD BECOME
BRIGHT.
PLEASE OH PLEASE, WHAT CAN I DO?
MY LIFE IS EMPTY WITHOUT YOU.
DO NOT LAUGH AT THE TALES OF MY STRIFE.
BUT GIVE RESPECT TO THE DEATH OF MY LOVE
LIFE.

Exodus

Who I am

I am an individual a part of a collection of individuals. I am one who strives for fantasy in the realm of reality. I look for the peculiar gene in people because this in my norm. I see not with my eyes, but with my heart.
Who am I?

I like to sit back and contemplate hard questions on life and the Creator. I read my Word and focus on the Goodness of my Almighty Parent. I wonder why have I been blessed with opportunities, spontaneity, humility and the thirst for unity through Him. I pray for a brighter sun and a cooler rain.
Who am I?

I am a sister that appreciated my blackness, my caramel colored skin, my manageable (yet processed) hair. My long eyelashes that flip on command. I am a queen that enjoys my dialect, which has now been categorized as EBONICS. I enjoy my taste in clothes, not grunge, not hip-hop, but clean. I love the wise words of a spiritual being; yet I am defensive toward philosophers who try to conceive negative teachings that I refuse to let my eyes and ears receive.
Who am I?

I am one who sees love. One, who acknowledges the existence of it, but always, mostly I am afraid to embrace it. Love, or so-called love, has bitten my hand too many times, when all I wanted to do was feed off its warmth, and companionship. Love played the role of lust; therefore, I was hurt by love's cruel sense of humor. Laugh love for I hate you. I love to hate you. I hate

to love you. I hate to be without you. Love can make one blind to the truth, but fear of love can make one a believer of falsehood, loneliness, and heartache. I would hate to live without love.
Who am I?

Basically a picture cannot explain who I am. What my thoughts are and the experiences I have endured. Pictures cannot tell my likes and dislikes and strengths and weaknesses, goals and past failures. Or can it? Is my word not painting a picture? Of a person who deals with life? Who doesn't run away from it? Sometimes words are who we are. Our picture. If one enjoys, despises, corrects my words, my picture, than feel free. As many beaches to the vast land. But beware dear reader, for you have been warned. That is…
Who I am.

8.11.1999

Dear Daddy,
It is funny that I haven't written to you in a while.
 I think back and I want to write of things profound and deep. But I can only write what comes to mind. Lately I have been inspired to explore the arts more.
 I know and understand that has been a part of me for a long time. It has been three days since my birthday passed.
I feel twenty.
Daddy, I feel very grateful. I am staying at my parents' house for a few days. I know that they needed to see me, but mostly I needed them. I am ashamed at the fact that I place a deceit to my being of being tough. I am. But I am composed of many emotions. I can honestly say that I love You so

29

much and I am looking forward to what You choose to do with my life. I know that my life is destined for greatness, which is why I am grateful. Lately, I have been going through some very difficult times.

I lost my job that I cared so much about, my beloved plant that seemed to be an extension of my soul has died, and my family has been experiencing times of poverty again.

Daddy, I know that You made me strong. But at times I don't understand. I praise You and play by all the rules, but yet my family lives in a place were masking tape is used to capture unwanted pestilence. The rats have left, but the hot water, necessities and healthy environment has left with them. The worst of it all is that our home is one of the better homes in the neighborhood. I can't let my people suffer. I beg of You, use me.

And do I feel bad when I return to my so-called paradise on the north side of Chicago? Sometimes. I feel that my prayers are not enough. I feel bad that I have been privileged and not worthy because of my kind fortune. I know that it is because of Your grace and mercy. It hurts, Daddy, so bad though. It seems as if all or most of my friends have been trapped. Either with early marriages, children, abortions, abuse, drugs, death, or worse, trapped in a limited poverty mindset. I am grateful because I have had the opportunity to eat of these fruits, and some I have added to my collection of delicacies, but still I am chosen, set apart.

I thank You

Dear Daddy,

I would like to apologize.

For all the things that were uttered from my lips.

But mostly for the things that I was thinking.

I got so frustrated.

I don't know how it got that far.

I am so sorry. I didn't want to hurt You.

I just didn't want to be me.

What you are asking seems hard to me.

I just need some help.

I know that I need some discipline.

Daddy,

I am so scared because I don't see this stuff.

I don't know anymore.

Do I need to retreat

from certain

company

that I

find

so

c

o

n

s

u

m

I

N

G

?

If I

must,

I will.

Please just teach me.

I have fallen in so many ways.

In love,

In rage,

In passion.

All these things seduce me and romance my soul.

I am weakened.

I know this, but fear that,

But for some strange reason I call this home also.

31

I refuse!

I refuse to be labeled as hoe,
slut, bitch, easy,
or any other term that does not define or express my
dynasty since birth.
I refuse
to allow those within my ever-so - guarded walls to
perceive me anything other than queen, daughter of
Zion,
beautiful,
set apart,
virtuous,
and not forgetting real.
I refuse to deny myself life's pleasure while
following the rules of the most High.
I am created,
designed for purpose,
destined for greatness,
and determined to get there.
I refuse to allow devils,
thieves, imps
and, or anything that tries to rise itself against the
knowledge of things prayed for,
sought after,
fasted for and or went to hell and back for,
be stolen, destroyed, raped
and or molested.
I refuse to let loose those dreams.
visions, promises.
I refuse to let my self,
my soul,
my spirit fall
and
or

fail.

Dear You,

I am so frustrated right now.
Everything that I wish to say to you always sounds
good in my head, but I can never get it out. Well, here
goes: I am upset with you. No. I am pissed at you,
now I feel that you are taking advantage of this
friendship. Today I asked you, told you to stop. But of
course you didn't. It was not the fact that we were
playing. The fact was and is that you were
disrespecting my stop. Oh, but the whole world has to
pay homage to you when you get in one of your
fucking moods. I am supposed to humbly kiss your
ass, and mean it, spew blood and basically suck your
dick in order for our friendship to be consistent. Is it
because I am a girl? That's bullshit. I love you, but
sometimes you are a real ass. See, you are one of the
closest people to me right now and I don't need added
shit in my life. It honestly makes me sad that my
family is in Florida and my friend feels like he can
expose, taunt, belittle and hurt me at his damn
amusement. That's not right. I know that I love you,
but do you love me like you say you do. God, I would
gladly spend the rest of my life with you, but I can't.
Not when my heart is literally broken. All I wanted
when I came up to the room was love. Maybe some
affection. Hell, I like to feel appreciated too. Why did
you lash out at me? You kicked me when I was down.
I understand that you have issues going on, but so do
I. Just like everyone else on the planet. Look at what I
am saying, how can we help each other? Am I even
helping? Do we need some time away from each
other? Do we need this to end? I don't know because I
am tired. Seriously, I am hurting; nobody understands
me, and everyone has left. I am here alone. I can
handle that if I have to. But if there is something to

33

salvage, let me know because I am tired. I am tired of the roller coaster emotions. I am tired of playing the role of your girlfriend at times. I am tired of the gray areas. I am just tired. I am tired of loving you and not knowing if you love me like I love you. Sometimes I wonder if there is a future with us. I do, you know.

Then a smile comes on my face. There is some comfort in knowing that you could be my friend for life.

I have written a lot. I had to get some things out. Excuse the language, but I am processing as I go. I don't want you to be afraid of me. I know that you have opened up more, and that needs to be praised, but it still hurts. Here I am, up at 4 o'clock in the morning writing to you a bitchy, love letter. I need clarity. I need to know what this is. You know, this thing we have. I need you to communicate and tell me. I don't have time for you to monitor your words, and or try to sugar coat things to spare my feelings. I need you. The holistic real you. Not saying that you haven't been showing me. You just have to be clear. You have to love me enough to let me go. Whatever you decide, know that I will support it. Tell me what you want because I want you. Tell me.

10.5.2000

Dear Daddy,

I first want to say that I apologize for not caring about our relationship,

For not spending time with You,

For doubting You, and for not putting You first.

I am sorry.

I have acquired a taste for sin.

I am being as real with You and with myself as possible.

34

I masturbated. I also thought of someone while I was
doing it.
Well, tried to.
This was before the beautiful phone call I got from
Iesha and Angel, and also before the Bible study.
Lord, I am lonely.
I sometimes feel like I need to be with someone. I
asked him one night recently that we should go out on
a date, a real one.
To make a long story short, he told me that he was not
ready.
I heard that and I respected that.
It hurt though.
I thought I was being rejected again, but I swallowed
my pride.

10.26.2000

Dear Daddy,
I'm here writing to You in the doctors' office.
I am here to understand what is wrong with me.
Physically.
I've been real emotional lately.
A lot of things have been hurting me.
I miss my family.
I'm upset about this Krishna issue.
I miss my father.
My money is low, and I am worried about my classes.
I don't write all of this down to just complain.
I wrote them down to find some truth.
Babes said something really important.
He said that the Bible speaks on how the truth will
make you free.
Well, the truth is that I am not alone, there are people
fighting with me.

35

The truth is that Krishna is dealing with things just like I am, and that I should be upset with the spirit behind it.

The truth is that my father Abraham loves me, and that he is dealing with whatever he needs to for this season, but he will be back.

The truth is that working makes your finances increase.

The truth is that this is the season for me to be in school, and the only way to get knowledge is to go to class everyday.

The truth is that I am a minister of You and I have to carry myself as such.

If I am a virtuous woman, I need to behave as such.

If I am a DJ, I need to behave as such.

Since I am set apart, I need to know You intimately.

I trust you Daddy, some things just hurt.

I refuse to doubt You again.

I love you Daddy, and I will trust whatever You are doing.

11.30.2000

Winter Break…

Dear Daddy,

As you know I am reading "Woman thou Art Loosed".

It is powerful.

I praise You for what you've inspired T.D. Jakes to write.

A lot of stuff inspired me, but the most powerful thing that spoke to my spirit was on page 121.

Genesis 2:21-25 refers to the creation of Eve, the first wife.

"She was created a woman while Adam was asleep."

That makes so much sense.

While a "thing" is being done he has to be asleep.

36

You are brilliant.
Not only do you create us from a piece of man,
You allow us to be transformed, created, recreated and
polished in secret.
You keep us covered.
Then you wake him or bring him to the realization of
the union after and only after your creation is
complete.
Thank you Daddy for hiding me while You are
perfecting Your creation.
Thank you for keeping him asleep.

1.8.2001

Dear Daddy,
It is a brand new quarter.
I am excited and motivated more than ever now.
I understand how important it is for me to get my
education,
So that is what I must do.
I pray that You help me.
And also let me remember to keep You first,
in all things.
I am not a failure.
I am not surrounded by failures.
I am destined for greatness and I will walk in it.
I see myself with excellent grades and I will not settle
or except anything less.
I love me.
Please keep me in your perfect peace
so I can endure those things that I need too.
For the glorification of Your kingdom.
This I do humbly vow and pledge.

<u>Who am I Part Two?</u>

Well here I am, composing to make this paper
interpret the inner realms of me. I remember back
when this thing was new to me, this thing called
Art.

     As I scratch my scalp to release those things
that has given birth in my soul, I find myself blank.
Why then I think? Maybe because I have solidified
my manifestations causing them to be stuck at the
very same door I'm asking them to walk through.
So now I am in need of patience. Wait, wait, and
wait.

     Examining myself to push back the
anxiousness and press forth the consciousness of
my being, and it arrives. My wants, my needs, my
desires, my insecurities all with their cups willing
and ready to drink from my passion. Eager in their
own garb.

Like breast milk to a young seed, each has and
instinctive decree to feed.
To be fed.
Feeding questions boiling in the housing complex I
like to call the heart.
Why am I a Jack of all but a master of none?
How come I can say I know you but sometimes
choose not too?
What do I do now, after our eyes met and sang
sweet sonnets that your lips refuse?
Preach girl, preach!
No nonsense, just some sense.
No nonsense, just two cents.
No nonsense, just sense of the truth.
I'm not who I will be.

And I ain't what I used to be.
Shhh… not deep, not deep at all.
Just real.
No I have not arrived.
Just real.
Who knew?

Mama said they'll be days like this. There'll be days
like this my mama said. Oh she said I'd be just like
this, I'd be just like this my mama said.

Who knew?

2.10.2001

Love and Ocean

Finally two worlds that have often glanced but never
spoke finally meet.
We are soul mates.
My dear friend where have you been?
Where have you been?

We are so a like, but very different.
Each ruler in our own dimension.
Even still I welcome you.
I do believe you were put here to cause completion.
Be not confused.
Not to my person, but to my purpose.
I am already whole.
All thanks to the Creator.
It is refreshing to finally see you and know that this road
we travel was pre-destined before the fall of the third.
You and I are here.
I admit I am eager to know the innermost, quietest place
of you. I even wish to visit your anger.
He is only fueled by passion.
Don't be afraid. He will not bite the hand that feeds him.

I feel compelled to warn you.
Some corners in my house are damp and polluted with
spider webs.
But trust and know that the foundation is strong.
The house will stand.
I will stand.
Un-moveable.

2.25.2001

Accountability

So you ask what to do after you hear spick, mutt, wop,
cracker, and nigger.
So you ask what to do after you've been followed in
the stores, seen as exotic, or disrespected.

"If you can't use their comb, than don't bring them
home."
"He's black, but he doesn't act black, you know
ghetto."
"You can talk to her, she's easy. You know what they
do."
"But they are all good in math."

Either how canst thou say to thy brother, Brother let
me pull out the mote that is in thine eye, when thou
thyself beholdest not the beam that is in thine own
eye…and then shalt thou see clearly to pull out the
mote that is in thy brother's eye (Luke 6:42).

Christian, you. You Christian
Catholic, Protestant, Jew, Gentile, Black, White, Red,
Brown, Yellow.
Christian. Christ-like.
Christian. Christ-like.

"The ism or understanding of being like
Christ."
"Jesus, What is the most important commandment?"
"Love the Lord God with all your heart, soul and mind
and love thy neighbor as thyself.

Love your neighbor as yourself.
So the real question is "how do I love me?"

Do I really love my eyes, my nose, ears, and mouth?
Do I really love my skin, cream, olive, cinnamon, and
many shades of chocolate?
Do I really love my hair, straight, wavy, kinky?

Because if I did, I would love yours.

Love thy neighbor as thyself.
Love your neighbor as your self.
        As yourself?
Him, her, she, he as yourself.
Catholic, Protestant, Jew, Gentile, Black, White, Red,
Brown, Yellow.
Christian. Christ-like.
        "The ism or understanding of being like
Christ."
Stand.

You Christian. Stand! Stand up and be accounted for.
Wake up and realize that it is not about you.
Stand up and realize that it's about the kingdom.

3.26.2001

Dear Daddy,

Hey. It's me of course.

41

Here I am crying again. Daddy, I truly need Your strength. You have told me some things that are quite scary. I come asking for help. I am constantly being hurt. Even with my so-called wise knowledge. The only reason why I hurt is because I know what I know. I don't know how long I can last. Please keep me in Your perfect peace. Please Daddy; your baby girl is hurting. You have commissioned some hard things of me and I am asking for your strength. I have become so-callused when it comes to issues with him. I am very confused. He is attracted to and sleeps with men, but he states that he is not gay. He is attracted to women, but never me. I am appalled. Not mostly because of these things, even though they do bother me, I am hurt that I still love him as much as I did before and strangely those feelings grow. Am I a fool? God, this is the man You said will be my husband? All these things are basically done in my face. I am tired of talking, crying, playing, and snotting over him. I need You, Daddy. I am hurt by the love that I have. It is hard to keep all of this inside. And it's going to get worse before it gets better. One thing that I can hold on to is that You are always faithful, and I trust You. I am just human and it just hurts. He is a great guy, though. Sometimes, I just wish that he will wake up. Sometimes he is so sleep. He is too bright, intelligent, wise and beautiful to be so stupid. Why in all of hell would you tell your closest girl friend, who has feelings about you, about another woman's breast? Why would someone do that? It would be easier to take a knife and stab me in the heart. I know he loves me, but sometimes I think that he doesn't think. So to hold on to the little bit of dignity that I had left, I asked him when he was going to sleep with her. I didn't ask him out of spite. I asked him to let him know that she gave him pictures of her, including those with nudity, as an invite. After that happened for a while, he stated, "How do you know that it hasn't already been done?" Why is he trying to kill me? Or trying to drive me crazy? I don't get it. Is he stupid or is he playing dumb? Or does he expect me to be stupid? Lord, I want him to either wise up or tell me to leave his life. I need relief from this crazy limbo land. I want to walk out. I want to leave. I want to move on with my life. I need to feel free. Lord, how will we come together? I know that it is only through Your will and Your power that this ministry will ever manifest. I just need You. Teach me what you want me to know. Please God, let me not be callused toward him. Please let me care and not be judgmental.

Teach me how to love him as his sister. Let the things that I go through bless someone else. Dry my tears. Heal my heart. Comfort me when I'm lonely. Let me not look for natural signs and wonders. Give me your love. Teach me how to love. Let me love him as his sister and friend full of agape love. And show me how to let You do what you need to do with that man. He is from You and even though he drives me up the wall, I know he loves me. And He loves You. Thank You for him.

4.1.2001

Why are you here?
I asked you why are you here?
Did you come to hear a tickling of the ear or a
caressing of the soul?
I tell you now, I never proclaim to be a prophet,
Performer,
Or even a poet.
But I come as a servant.
Here to breath life into those areas that has been
murdered,

Or victims of suicidal situations.

So,

I ask you.

Why are you here?

4.20.2001

Battle

"I'm on the battlefield for my Lord. I am on the battlefield for my Lord. See I promised that I will serve Him till I died and I'm fighting, fighting for the Lord..."

See, I always knew that I was called to be a soldier.
I knew that my time was near; I was presented with
the opportunity to fight. See, this is different from
those tiny increments of conflict; I was going on the
front line. I was going to war. I think I'm ready.
See, I got my gun, I know all the drills, and I've
seen the effects on faces prior to.

I fought before - not like this, but definitely before.
I had to survive on army rations and make clothes
from the throw-a-ways, oh, I mean hand me downs,
of curses passed on my lineage. I survived. I painted
my face with the camouflage of yester year's
relationships. And I pulled my hair back so that
when my enemy saw me, he thought that I was he,
therefore, trusting me. And as he turned I took my
knife and slit his throat. I watched love's blood pour
frantic and nauseous. I didn't wait to see if he was
dead or alive. But I did see his eyes. And in a brief
moment a lesson was taught to me with patience. I
have, I did, somehow, cut myself.

I ran, and ran deep into the obis of me all the time
screaming sanctuary as if I was a Notre Domical

hunch back. I ran, then walked, and crawled to a place that granted me safe passage. I entered, I slept, and I healed.

I met others like me. Some fatly fed with knowledge that spoke to my situation. I was grateful and extremely appreciative, but all in all they, too, were in this place of refuge. Away from the war.

Within myself I knew that the time would come that I would be summoned to fight again. As my soul boiled, waiting in anxiousness, my entire being sang the melody of tick tocks. Waiting for the alarm of my dawning.

Finally my letter arrived. My captain oh captain has located me. Because I healed in a timely fashion I was commissioned to fight again.

Walking forward on a road once traveled in reverse, I begin to mentally check my inventory. Herbs, check, spices, check, candles, check, sweet songs, soft nothings, deep something's, intimacy, ecstasy, spirituality, talents, passion, tears, smiles, oil, me, my all, my self, check.

Knife, check!

I was equipped with all the things I know now I needed in earlier battles. Accompanied with tools used prior to.

I built my fort along the riverbank. I can see him when he comes. I reply to my captain that I accept his mission and sent my coordinates.

I waited; I'm scared, apprehensive, ready, and even fearful of my enemy. My tactics before have failed because my enemy is still alive. And even stronger. I prepare.

My fort is fashioned with brick and granite. Only the sun and moon can enter and exit without permission.

I prepare. I look, I guard, I patrol. I recite the law. I surrender myself. I render burnt offerings. I present myself. A living sacrifice.

"I will sing praises, praises unto you."

Surprisingly while I wasn't looking my enemy snuck in and shocked hell out of me. He took his dagger, stabbed me in the heart and laid me on the paved floor of my own fortress. My red blood flowed from my body as if at Niagara. He knelt down and cried tears of agony. His weeping covered my body, filled my heart, and anointed my soul.

My enemy was my inner me, and therefore covered and filled me as he entered me with all intensity.

So I write. My last will and testimony. I leave all those things that were learned to those still in captivity or safe in the arms of sanctuary. I die only to be reborn.

My slayer known as my enemy really revealed to be my ally. He freed me from the death of routine. Thus, slain my love.

Hello Sir

How are you? I just stopped to say that you have made my day, and my face is now greeted with a smile.

How are you? It is very rare that my eyes glare and stare at a beauty so divine. To sit and reflect and respect this man whose love I wish was mine.

"You are fine." you replied, even though you didn't have to tell me because I see you, and what I see pleases my eye. I'm talking about your soul, your passions, and those things you hold dear. Those things that drew me nigh.

As your lips part to slice through the shallow forepaw, you pour your heart to me. Oh how privileged am I to know and feel and relate to sounds, words, stories, life, that is so complex and free.

Hello

I will start like any member of the masses by stating my name. It is Talonie Starr. Sometimes it is easier for me to write it phonetically. I am an individual with many levels. Some of which I enjoy facing. The others are closely related to programs seen on Science Fiction Theater.

I grew up on the south side of Chicago. I am the second youngest of seven. My childhood can be very gray. When reflecting on my past, I envision myself walking in a dark, damp basement. In the distance I see light piercing from under a door. As I press for that refuge, I feel the thin webs from spiders on my face. Even though the smell is of concrete and mildew, I find it pleasing. It is familiar. I am hesitant and even fearful, but I walk on.

As I look at myself now, I see someone very grand. I see someone clothed in humility and armed with authority. I am the beginning stage of a mosaic beam. I am placed in position to be a beautiful foundation. I want to be complete. I want to be someone's muse.

4.20.2001

I dream of a place where he and I are in love…

…And he comes to me and looks me in the eye and says, "You are my mirror. You and I are one." That day will come when he and I are I and I. So I continue to write. I write about his lips, his eyes, and his breath against my brow. I love him. I wait for him in my dreams. This is a place of lodging for our love. It keeps no boundaries and it knows no fears. Funny how this piece of paper gets to hear my innermost thoughts that my lips fail to utter. My only wish is that your lips articulate and translate the message that your eyes speak. Honestly, sometimes I feel betrayed. I can feel myself boil with anger. Can't you smell my passion? How can you reject, reject, eject me. You push me away, your soul mate. God has placed us here to fore fill that ministry. So please understand the plight of my pain. We complete each other's purpose. Oh, my love. I was writing love songs about us before I uttered your name. I must confess. In all of my excitement and anxiousness, I told of the vision. I spoke of a secret given from the heavenliest on many an ear. I know that this has given much pain. Instead of keeping the promise and holding the vision, in secrecy, like the beloved Virgin, I told and settled for the ridicule of being perceived as mad. There was a time once when someone whose blood runs the same as yours confessed to you this secret. I was frightened that you would run away. I am glad that you didn't. I think too much. Sometimes I sit and think about you. I wonder if you are missing me. I wonder if you dream dreams of another life or that which lies in the future. Can't you see them? Those pitter-patter are replicas of your feet. Look, she has your hair and eyes. He bares your name. And he looks like one of your ancestors. That is my reason for not dating. Now that I have seen my Adam, why should I settle?

Summer of 2001

Dream

…There was a choir engagement. I didn't have the proper uniform. I went shopping. Babes was with me. He was asking me to buy all this stuff that I couldn't afford. He had left, leaving behind his planner and bag. I went after to follow. I ended up on 63rd and Morgan, at the old church. I was praying like Job had prayed. I looked over and all of my belongings were on fire. I was mourning. There was a glove were the index finger was made of steal. I could smell the passing of the rain. I hid under a table. As I closed my eyes and bit into a potatoes that was lying on the ground. When I opened them, I was in a house. I walked up the stairs emotionally troubled. My friend Kris accompanied me up these stairs. I told

54

her of my story, of how I was wet, hungry and
homeless. I didn't have anything. She told me
to not tell anyone. While upstairs, I could
see through my mind's eye how people
downstairs were talking about me. Saying
things that implied that I was crazy. "Don't
believe anything she says." This dream was
full of color. All of my senses were alert. I
was hungry and crying. …

When I woke up I was hearing the gospel song by
Fred Hammon 'My Heart Depends'
I told Babes that night. I had to wake him. He asked
me why I was crying. I muttered, because I was
alone. No one believed me, everyone left my life. I
had no one, nothing. It hurt. It was my biggest fear.
To exist and no one knew.

7.14.2001

<u>Love Song</u>

I sing of a love song. I sing of a love song where I

am allowed to be me, and you're free to be. With

earth, with sky, water, fire and always including me

in the matrimonies orgy of three.

I sing of a love song where we leave dilapidated

words to die and communicate with our eyes and

our touch. I sing of a song of freedom. Love me, sex

me, and feel me in the fifth dimension.

I sing of a love song. My song consists of meters, measures, and beats, rhythms, symbols and soul. It chimes and quotes the patterns of your heartbeat. You know it hurts me to know you while you think you know me. If so, sing my song. Know the world of the words as if you were in the presences of Jill Scott. Or better yet, sing the song that motivated that lady that sang the blues.

I sing of a love song. I sing a song where poets lived what they preached and where pussy poetry was left to woo one's partner. Not just to obtain passage into those pearly gates decorated with calry shells and perfumed with essential oils, basically pussy.

I sing of a love song before it was watered down to a "We are the World" speech. When folks was happy to be nappy. And where we stopped using our darkest skinned brothers and sisters as rites of passage to the motherland.

I sing of a love song because I'm tired of singing a song of envy, pity, hopelessness, oh yeah jealousy.

I sing of a love song because, Hell, because it's time. My song consists of pain, tears spawned from experience, birth through fear. I love you. My song consists of kisses, hugs, etc., etc. Why do I have to pay a stranger to stroke my locks? But you say you know me. If so, sing my song. Know the worlds of the words as if you are in the presence of Anita Baker. Oh better yet, sing the song that motivated the queen of soul.

I sing of a love song. I sing of a song where people were not afraid to love you more, and refuse to stay in the comfort zone of friendship, because it's comfortable. My song consists of broken chains and rusted locks. It consists of liberation in the heart. Every orifice of you body yells your declaration that your punk ass lips deny. Punk ass lips. Tell them bastards to be quiet. The chaotic noise that they produce is stifling and choking the tasty and tantalizing message of your essence. If life and death are in the power of the tongue, then right now I ask you to speak both by saying nothing. But sing to me, with me a song that is outside the mis-communicator of speech and fly with me outside time. But will you? I know you have the strength to. You dream dreams where you take up wings and swim through the many shades of the Borealis. Or will you be bond by the perception of fear painted across your punk ass lips. Damn, it hurts me to know you while you think you know me. If so, sing my song. Know the worlds of the words as if you where in the presences of the great Minnie Rippleton. Or better yet, sing the song that motivates the queen of gospel.

I sing of a love song. I sing of a song that lovers sing at sunset, a baby sings while cradled in a bosom, and the cry of achievement. I sing of a song that kept the melody to Negro spirituals. My song is made up of new fallen dew, summer rains, and cool breezes. My song chimes like electricity exciting and igniting every hair follicle. It runs deep like that stream within the ocean, and blesses like a rose, with or without that name would still smell as sweet.

I sing of a love song. I sing of a song that has life of its own. It prays that it penetrates your outward shell of flesh. It prays that you use all your so-called knowledge to decipher the cipher it spits to you. Take your blinded eyes to read in between the lines to receive the message birth for you. But come correct, because it will check, if you disrespect, despite reject the piece that is before you. Because you might catch a thrusting fist, and bruise those things I call your punk ass lips.

I sing of a love song because I am tired of talking. My words go in one ear, out the other, down your shoulder, eventually hitting the ground. You utter, "Oops, did I accidentally step on that?" You knew what the hell you were doing. Clumsy ass feet. Stepping on my heart and my passion. A weaker woman would have been turned in her resignation. So I sing. My song consists of God motivating me to keep on, push further. To believe, in love for you and for my love song.

But you think you know me. If so sing my song. Know the worlds of the words as if you were in the

presence of Kim Burrell. Or better yet, sing the
song that motivated the woman that gave you life.
Or even better, start my song before I begin.

MOOD OF MINE IN THE MORNING

I sit back
      And think
      And breathe
      And acknowledge
The many moods of mine.
And at first I am blank with nothing
To recollect or remember.
But as I started to write.
I cannot help but to think about my mood in the
morning.
For one, I am not a morning person
And for two, my morning is my time of rest.
Now I know
      And understand
      And pity those who join the masses at
            6 o'clock AM
To please a taskmaster.
But I am one who plays the game but by my own
rules.
      "Pass go, collect $400."
If one chooses to start their day at the crack of
dawn, I don't have a problem with it at all.
      But?!
When one chooses to conform me to a brainless,
      Motor skill depending,
      Coffee drinking,
      Agenda keeping,

Bureaucratic,
American,
I tend to get a little angry.
Rage fills my eyes like rushing water breaking
through a dam.

My heart hardens like water thrown on glass in sub-
degree weather.

My mind is clouded with words that the sailors use
in taverns.

But then I return to my right mind
       And focus.
       Think,
       And listen,
To what is going on.
I remember my sanity and control my emotions,
               Sometimes.
I wake up not because of pleasure,
       But because of obligation.

Moods of Sound

Are you in as much awe as I am? Do you hear what
I hear? Can you feel each persistent prayer with
each note? Can you feel that calm cool breeze with
every chaotic composition? I feel afloat. I am
impressed. I thank God for the privilege to

understand and appreciate the passion of music, of ministry. Even still every declaration of victory over trials, tribulations, heart aches and breaks are being made clear to my soul. My Abba, I thank you for an ear to hear and a mind to know and love those things in its purity, music.

Continue to breath.

11.3.2001

The Story of Mary Magdalene

I speak of a story of intimates and truth. I tale that speaks of love, envy and pain. I speak of a story, for me, which has no end. That would be the tale of Mary Magdalene. It would be unjust to speak on her behalf, so I speak, as I best know. To tell the tale of love and pain. And the seeds that Mary did sow. It will not be long or cause slumber to the flesh. But revive and give life to the season I call a test. So look alive and hear of a story, for me, which has no end. It contains a love affair from a foul able woman named Mary Magdalene.

She speaks to me through pages of life that I hold so dear. She danced and pranced for crowds, or people who were near. But life stood still when she met a man deemed to save her soul. This made her life and actions speak of love that needs to be told. That man was her God, savior on earth. To him she had to adhere. Even though her life was not as right, her love was shown so clear. Towards the eve of his death, one she knew that would come, she embraced him without thrust of hand or cheer. She took her myrrh encased in Alabaster and poured it on his head. Covered his feet with oil and tears. From her hair was made a bed. Then after this sincere touch of love she covered his feet with her body, coiled to make the sentiment clear. That she loved him because he loved her. The gratitude was dear.

Sadly the first words that were spoken were to ridicule her. See, such actions are misinterpreted by the blind. But the final words were spoken by her love. Who defended her beauty, how kind?

I speak because I prayed to Him to relate to me. And as simple and complex as God is,

She whispered like a warm summer breeze.
You wish to know of your purpose, for you,
which seem to have no end. Then find favor
with a woman who knows pure intimacy,
Her name was Mary Magdalene.

Winter of 2001

Well, dreams do come true. Now homeless while in college. Now, I am a senior, I am a

To be or Not...

I was thinking back to a time where your eyes saw me. It reminded me of a story I heard. Great North African Gurus' tell of stories of the pyramids. They say that they are perfect in design. And in the right time of year, the sun kisses the top of the pyramid and its' beauty can be seen from lands unheard of. It draws strangers to partake in the fellowship of knowledge and love. I see those same wonders in your eyes. I see and feel the current of the Nile with every glance. But it is because I see this I must tell you no. There are so many things that are missing from Cleopatra's story.

It began many years ago. I was one who thought I had a concept of love. I repeated the lies told to me with evil touches and spells from the dark. In my youth I acquired an immunity to even the most venomous of snakes and I survived. I went to a place of sanctuary and asked for safe passage to heal and not hurt. I learned tactics and gave praise in order to subdue my disease. Unfortunately, in order to become immune you are often a carrier. I carried this plague.

I met a man in my freshmen year of college. Or at least he was in the shell of one. He was a caramel colored guy whose height reached a towering level of five foot seven. His body also resembled that of a Roman god. He was thick and tight. Anthony was my friend. We did everything and said anything. He was I and I was he. This is how I found out that he loved me and two other women. I blame no one but myself. See I gave him permission into my heart. I let him in. Even to this day- I confess- I think about the tales of "what ifs?" Something inside me needed him. I blinded myself to the fact that he loved me but not only me. I closed my eyes to the fact that the girl he wanted to carry his last name was not me, Lover X. I ignored the fact that the girl who was carrying his child would not carry his last name, and that even she was not me, Lover Y. I hated the fact that I ignored all of my teachings and tactics and praises given to subdue this devil in order to satisfy my physical self.

I was wrong. I knew it. I didn't care. I decided that I had been a victim for so long that it was time for me to victimize. So what he was cheating on his fiancé? So what she was a sixteen-year-old pregnant girl? So what we all went to the same place of worship? I did not care that I called them all friend.

I was in too deep. I dealt with it.

Anthony worked by my school. I was a Chicagoan, straight A student, poet, alto in my gospel choir, tall, electric, fire wire who had access to whatever. It was easy for me. He would come by my dorm in the morning before class, at lunch, after work, spend the night, until the morning visits consisted of me kissing him goodbye to go to work. His fiancé, who thought I was her friend, would call and ask to speak with him while we were cradled in each other's arms. After a while I didn't even see the other girl, Lover Y, who was ashamed to attend Sunday morning service because of fear of being ridiculed. I'd created a monster.

If only I could make it stop. If only God could hear my cries to end this evil I had placed on the world. If only I cared. If only the thrill did not excite me so. I remember the very first time we had, or made…. It was like I wasn't even myself. While seducing each other, we knew the consequences. We knew about all the people that we would hurt, but our wills were enraged with passion. With every breath came death and rebirth. I wanted my own crucifixion. I fantasized about the alter being my place of nesting. I had decided that I was the devil incarnate, and for this I must recreate the fall of the third. I was an angel who had lost all right and privileges to sit before God and adore His feet. My wings were broken. My only resolution was death.

After we had finished, it was like our eyes had opened. I knew what it felt like to be naked in Eden. I knew why Eve ran from the voice of the Lord. The fruit was good, too good, too delicious, and yet poisonous. So I ran. I did not get very far. I went to my drawer and I opened it. My flesh wanted redemption. I looked for the thin, shiny blade I used to arch my eyebrows. I wanted to arch my wrist. I wanted the blood to flow on the carpet. I knew Christ himself allowed his blood to flow in order to establish repentance. It had to work again.

Funny, I never found that blade. I don't know if I moved it or if it had divinely disappeared. All I know is that it was one of those things that just was.

Anthony, my friend, the guy I called brother, the guy I made my lover, was over in the corner bawling tears. His weeping was as if a mother who was breast-feeding her child suddenly died. He saw me looking for something. He knew what I was looking for. He knew what I would do. He ran over to me. He begged me to live. He asked me to pray. I answered "for what?"

Something that day died in me. I became a new creature. I was Rosemary's baby. I lived off of others' emotions like a parasite. And after a while, my wounds began to show. Many whispered at church about what was happening, but they really didn't know. Yes, the church saw the linger of premarital sex, but did they see the face of the devil? The entities that knew how to create evil but could never win the war in the end? Did they really see what I was showing them?

It went on for months. I had become cold in order to numb others feelings towards me. I never spoke a word of it. Until one day my suite mates asked me a question regarding orgasms and I decided to tell the truth. This was how they found out that I was with him. This was when I began to feel. I was exposed.

In my room I had this sign:

> "While in this room, please refrain from cursing, smoking, drinking, and/ or basically anything that would disgust the Holy Spirit."

After I shared this vital information, one of them ran over to the wall and ripped it down in front of my face. She looked at me with eyes of satisfaction, like I finally belonged. I violated the intended meaning on the sign. She said with a Grinch-like smirk, "You will not be a hypocrite."

When she tore that piece of paper off my wall I felt my heart rip. Now, I don't really know about the afterlife and being immortal, but I was one who can attest to the fact that it is possible to die and be reborn over and over and over again. Even though I knew what I was doing, I knew what I really loved. I knew what truly gave me peace and happiness. Even though that piece of paper had no power on its own, it reminded me of sanctuary. It said that I would not always be this way. I will not always be a poison. It was my light that guided me home while I was in the darkness. Now that it was in pieces I was lost. My candle blew out. I was finally sent to Hell.

Life is funny sometimes. While I was in the wilderness I wasn't thinking of anyone. I didn't know how to love. I just wanted to go home. I wanted to feel. I wanted to be a good person. I wanted to be a good friend. I wished to cry tears. I wanted to be a good Godparent to Lover Y's beautiful little girl, who I called Angel.

As time went on, I was alone. That was okay for me. I got past the birth of Angel. I lived through the wedding I was not invited to. I was even victorious in the inadvertent offer from Anthony to become a mistress. Life was turning around. And I wasn't afraid of exposure anymore.

I say life is funny because it is, now that I know how to live. But this existence is very new to me. I don't want to screw up. Since God is all-powerful and all -knowing, He knew how the devil would turn out. I think when he made me; He wanted to give me the knowledge of the universe, thus placing within my heart Heaven and Hell. Like Cleopatra, I, too, was powerful. I hear she loved. She conquered. She was conquered by love. In all this time she lived, in a tower and decorated with shells of perfection, with wondering eyes gazed at perfected pyramids, longing for balance. I need to know my balance. I know that whichever one I choose to love will be the one that will influence how I show it.

A perfect pyramid is equal, regardless of the side it falls on. It is completely geometrically balanced, perfect. If this is to be true, the great pyramid that stands next to the sphinx stands with regal beauty, yet stands flawed, imperfect.

3.2.2002

Dream...

...A group of friends and I arrived at my old junior high school. We were there to tutor some students, but we weren't supposed to be there, not at that moment. We stumbled into the auditorium. The room was filled with conversations. It was time to leave. In order for one of the men to get comfortable, the host on stage hypnotized him saying, "I am going to make him think he has the wings of an eagle." I found that humorous. Something was up. I knew it would be a spell. So, I protected the people around me and myself through prayer. I still was looking over at the event to see all it's happenings. The host said "the crucifixion" as the guy was already moving frantically, his arms flew back forcing his body to fold in half. Like a dancer's moves gone wrong. Everyone in the audience was so amazed that the performance went so well, not seeing what really happened. I said, "That's okay, yup that's witchcraft, they casting spells. I'll be cool as long as my friends and I are fine." The auditorium was colossal. There were people dancing in the

70

*aisle spraying something on the on-lookers. I
was busy thinking that I was in the mist of a
Wicca ceremony. My thoughts grew and grew and
as soon as I stopped thinking they all looked
at me. I had a long, flowing tube in my hand
and I was swinging it in a circular motion. As
I was swinging it in the air, it was breaking
the spell cast on me, protection. I look
behind me to put some on my friend, but it was
too late, he was under. As soon as I was
getting close to him, he walked away. I was
now sitting in a tight stairway aligned with
the wall in the room with my back to the
audience. They didn't want me to see. I
finally ran out of water. They were chanting,
moving closer to me. One bound my hands. I
couldn't move. He was finishing the spell on
me...*

When I woke up, I thought I saw someone sitting on my bed with his back towards me. I didn't know if it was a demon or my friend. It felt weird, yet familiar. Then I thought, real loud, "Don't be out of position, and be in position."

3.18.2002

Dream...

*...I was at my junior high school. I was
standing by a locker. If I ventured out, I
always went back to this same locker. I seemed
to be looking for something that I might have
left. I was with some young girls and I was
teaching them that Destiny's Child gospel
medley. I looked down and noticed that I was
wearing missed matched shoes. I went back to
the locker and someone mentioned that my shoes
were at the bottom of a stairwell. I walked
down the stairs and I ventured into a house
with many rooms. There were children playing
in one of the rooms. My mother and I were both*

there. My eyes noticed one girl in particular.
The room suddenly began attacking the
children. The swing that was carrying the girl
was pulled and she hit her head on the
ceiling. She began to run. My mother and I ran
after her. All of us were in 'old school'
nightgowns. We were chasing her throughout the
rooms, each room doing more horrible things to
her. My mother stopped and told me not to
follow her anymore. My mother went to her room
and grabbed a bottle of rubbing alcohol. I
thought that we were going to use the alcohol
in prayer and kick whatever spirits present
out. We went to the room the girl was in, my
mother first than me. The girl had transformed
into her adult self. She could have been me.
Next to her were two ghost faced, little black
boys. It was the opposite of black face. Their
eyes and mouths had no definition. When I saw
them, my body got a chill. My mother gave me
the alcohol, pulled me back, told me not to
follow her, and as she was holding my hand,
she began to say the Lord's Prayer…

I woke up. My body still had that chill. Like you are
in a dark room, by yourself, and someone comes out
and frightens you, chill. I prayed, repented, sang
songs, read the Lord's Prayer and called a friend.
As I was describing the boys to her, I got the same
chill.

Sun Apr 21 17:56:08 2002

Hey You,

I am writing this out of pain and hurt. I apologize in

advance if it offends you but I really wish that you

continued to read it, and also respond to it as

truthfully as possible. It started right before

72

thanksgiving. This was when our friendship was changing for the worse. I knew that in that summer and the fall quarter it was hard for us to see each other because I lived in Island Lake. I loved our visits and I know that the travels were difficult for you. Thank you for your sacrifice.

I really don't know what happened. One night after Mya's show. You were tired. I was playing. You got frustrated. I got a pillow pressed on my face. You went to sleep. I was being tortured. I woke you up. You heard my grips. Later, I saw you not trusting yourself or me on how to relate, touch, respond, and be real with me. I believe that this is when you started to let me go. Or at least that is how I felt.

I went out with this guy. His name was Paul. You and Barbette were getting me ready to go out that night. My wardrobe, make up, and hair was done. My shoes were off though. You took your time to decorate my hand with rhinestones. It was a flower I believe. But that night you seemed cruel. There were constant rebuttals of "shut up", nasty eye roles and quick derogatory comments. My heart excused it as petty jealousy. And in my insecurities I took your harsh words, lied to myself, and turned them into "You look beautiful's", and "I know that this is your first date but don't be nervous cause Barbette and I will be there's."

Then, on December 1st, I was put out. I was now experiencing the very thing that you endured, had been enduring since April. I knew you would understand. I thought back on the time when we were hungry and we ate, not well, but we were full and we were friends. But at Mike's it was different. We both were so wounded and so selfish that our own needs were all we saw and cared about. We began attacking each other. We parted ways.

Being that it was never resolved, we were so confused about the other's feelings. It was just easier for both of us to retreat. Hoping that if this friendship were to be than God himself would have to come from heaven to fix it and make it right. Our arms were too tired of trying to hold on and fight all at the same time. It was easier to stop, step back and turn around.

It was hard for me during that time. I was so angry with you. I felt annoyed and jealous. I was upset that your stuff was at your mother's and mine was in storage. I hated that you could sleep at your mom's and I had to stay with your sister and A&O. I hated that you had a car that you could escape to, or use to escape from, and I had a suitcase that I lived out of. I hated that you could be by yourself in the space of your car if you chose/had to sleep outside. I hated that I felt that you left me, and deep down I knew that even you had to survive.

In January, I got my place with the Murphy's. It was a little space, but it was mine. I really missed you. And all the great times we had. You were my friend, my buddy, my brother, and my family. I was apprehensive though. I didn't want to act like everything was okay, but I wanted to help you.

February, you got your place. I was so happy for you. I really was rejoicing. We were starting to talk and things were getting better. It was still uncomfortable for the both of us though. I respect that. In my happiness I was waiting on you to say, "Talonie, if you ever need a place to retreat, "or" where I am that is where you could be", to come out your mouth. But they never came. This affected me, but what was more painful was that it let me know that you were still holding ill feelings towards me.

March was getting better. I tried to keep my distance. Of course it wasn't always successful. I am sorry for that. I am sorry for that time that I invaded your space. I felt that as a friend I should be willing to sacrifice myself for your comfort. I didn't know what to do because I felt that you didn't tell me what you needed or didn't need from me. My fast was ending; I learned a lot of things. And I honestly feel that God prepared me for a lot of the stuff I was about to go through. I do thank God for this friendship though. In my relationship with you I have grown so much. I have learned plenty about myself. So thank you for being. One of the things I notice about myself was that I had trust issues and jealousy issues.

After Barbette's show, I told you about some of the things I was feeling. I wanted you to talk to me. I hate it when you hold stuff in. This stuff later turns to bitterness toward me and I am looking like, "what just happened?" but it is from stuff long ago. As you see I am also guilty of this. Sometimes, I didn't think you cared or wanted to know. After all of our turmoil, I thought that I was gone from your life forever. I see that I was wrong. I know that you cared deeply but like me afraid of the outcome, afraid of being attacked or taken for granted, afraid that I didn't care, and tired of trying. I respect you so much. I applaud you for being my friend this long. I know that it hasn't been easy. This is probably also due to the fact that I began to love you romantically, and you could not reciprocate that to me.

Wednesday of last week, you told me that you were dating Mya. Thank you for telling me. To be honest, it hurt me like a motherfucker. I still do have feelings for you. I can't deny that. I immediately started ragging on myself. I thought at first that you never loved me because you couldn't, but I see that you can love. So it had to be me. I thought that it was because of our current dramas personally and collectively. I thought it was because my grandparents didn't come from an island; therefore, I would never be cubano, puertoricano, bohemian, etc. I thought that it was because I was not a person that was on stage in the limelight. Then, I thought that I was not pretty enough, which is probably why you hardly gave me a compliment? Or maybe I was too tall? Or maybe I challenge you too much? Or maybe that you loved me so much that you knew that if you got in a relationship with me that you would have to be damn near perfect? Or maybe I was too perfect? Or maybe I had so much shit in my life that you did not have the time too deal with me? Or maybe you just had chemistry with Mya that was never there with me?

I know that I asked you a number of times as to why we were friends. Sometimes I wanted to hear "Because God ordained it", or "Because our love is pure and we feel and help each other." I confess that I feel like a fucking idiot when I think back to some of our encounters between March 20th and now. If I had known you two were together, I would not have poured out my heart. Not to somehow win your love, but to respect her and you by not complicating the situation. I would have shut the hell up about being replaced because I was never in that space to begin with. I just deleted the email that you sent to me the day before you made a commitment to her. At times I do want you to say "Talonie, leave me the fuck alone, and stay the hell out of my life." I wanted you to say, "I will never be in love with you and I wish you let me go." I know it may sound stupid, but I am being as real as possible while I am exposed and naked. When I processed what you told me I damn near had a heart attack. Parts of me felt like you lied to me when you told me you loved me. When I came back from my trip and we held each other because you missed me and I you, and you heard my stories about the rainbows (by the way the postcard has been sitting in the post office box since the 31st). And the pager voice mails, and your eyes asking me questions about my family, and asking people about me to see if I am okay. Other parts fight and tell me that it was sincere. That you love me. That only if there was a way that you can show it and not get wounded in the process. Or that I won't confuse it with you being in love with me. But this damn near killed me. But it would have done more damage if you never shared it. I know it wasn't easy. I know you didn't mean to hurt me. I am very grateful that you told me. Either way it goes, like you said, there was going to be hurt anyway. The fact that you shared it tells me that you still love and care about my well-being.

I know that this letter is long. Hell, I knew it was going to be long when I started it. But I felt that as your friend, you deserve the truth. The truth about me and the truth of how I feel. I did not mean to offend, cause any hurt or complications. I just wanted to get it all out on the table. I am not perfect but it doesn't excuse my actions. I know that. I pray that you see the sincerity behind it. I do love you. I will still be there. I respect your quest for truth. I respect your need for space and time. I love Mya and I wish you both blessings and prosperity. I hope you find what you are looking for and I pray that if she can help, that she will, and that you let her in long enough to do so. You are a beautiful person inside and out. It is no wonder why so many people want to be in your presence. I am blessed that you are in my life and I pray that I somehow blessed or inspired you. I do ask of you two things. Please pray for me regardless if you think that they are working or not. And PLEASE respond to this, communicate through email or telephone or even in person, but please don't sit on this!

Love,
Talonie

The Ability to Understand

Recently I had a dream that I was walking down this pathway. There were tall trees, low grass and the air was filled with the smell of fresh flowers. The wind was blowing gently and the sun was beaming warmth on to my face. In the distance of the path was a figure. As I got closer I noticed that it was a woman. I approached her. "If you go further, you will come across numerous gifts that will show you your future." Honestly, I got scared. Did I really want to know? With some hesitance, I went on.

I encountered the first gift. It was marked FAMILY. As I opened it, there were pictures in it. Of people, places, children, etc. I was overwhelmed. Could this really be my family? Suddenly, it began to fade away. I got scared. I went to the next box, and the next. Each box marked with concerns, wants, passions, talents, needs. And each faded.

Seriously upset now. Disturbed that everything that I touched disappeared. I went back to the woman. Highly pissed with tears raining down my face. I asked her, why was I able to see these things and not be able to have them. "Sometimes one needs to see what they are going to be in order to remember who they are and also what they were. But realize that progress is the most important, not things. And in all things there are appointed times and seasons."

And suddenly, for the first time, I woke up.

I wish the voices would choose to sing sometimes.

Que
Dien
te
Benisse

Some times I think of you. Well I lied, often times I think of you. I chose not to write for a long time because I thought it wasted my time. Sometimes, I don't know. I know that I am writing in code, but one day, maybe, you will understand why. I hear the songs that you compose. I like to think that the one you look for is me.

I lied. I am not over you. My secret that is known to the world is that I love you. I've loved you since forever. Sometimes what we look for is right in front of us. To be honest, I ask myself why I was inadequate. What was it that made me not be the one? I wish this were something that you could answer. As pathetic as it sounds, I ask for closure: what was it that repelled you from me?

I wanted to replace this love that I have for you with another. No one compares. I wonder sometimes if you hide your love for me. I don't know how to ask you without you running away. I am so horrible with myself sometimes. I allow things that you have said to me to stay a while and torture me. I remember you saying that you thought about us being together but… Or that it is easier to date someone who you are not intimate with because, if it fails it will ruin the intimacy. So inadvertently you seek out shallow relationships. I know that I am being random. My love for you surpasses me. I would say, allow yourself the pain of being loved and in love. The funny thing in this: since I am writing this, I know that we are not quite ready for each other. Maybe you have been wiser than me? Maybe I don't give you enough credit? Maybe you suffer for my love just as I for yours? Maybe you love me so much that you are waiting for you? What ever it is I feel that our love, even in its premature state right now is divinely cosmic. Being in relationship with you has allowed me to know what it means to be Christ-like. Please see how beautiful you are. This is pass your looks and talents. See how strong you are when you are weak and vulnerable.

7.21.2002

Vaya Con Dios

I know that this is hardly the place and the time, but I need to release. I love my people, culture, and even the African American church. I just wish that everything wasn't so routine. I think that I have somehow wasted my time. When do we step away from the church hats, church faces, the religious "praise the Lord saints" that come out without feeling, passion or zeal? How can we get away from being self-absorbed to retreat to the place where we first knew You? When things were simple, and all we knew was that You were, are and is God, and all that we needed, wanted, desired to do was be in Your face.

8.1.2002

Here I am. In a familiar scene, in a familiar situation. I am a diva at another poetry set, open mike soirée. As I breathe in the hot air, grateful that I wasn't asked for five dollars, I am wondering why I am here. Am I here because I like the scene, being in the mist of artists, my realm of comfort, ability and insecurity? Am I here because I wanted to get out? Or am I here because of him? After all the things I have said and felt, I am once again in a situation where I am supporting him. Go figure…

8.1.2002

Still Summer

…It is funny what you do while in love. Hell. It has grown me, cut me, killed me, restored me all to do it all over again. What is this scene? Are there others out there, in here, like me? Will I suffer the typical fate of an artist, letting my suffering speak through

86

my talents to only bless and mature others, only if I allow myself to suffer. For example…

I write mostly about love, only to be in love with a being that does not, cannot, reciprocate it. But yet, he loves to lie in it, as if it was a supple breast full of milk, drinking. And I sit, often times wounded from lack of affirmation, yet dying from trying to withhold my love from him.

I know the situation. I may even or possibly predict the outcome. Even still, I search. I search for his eyes to speak symphonies of I love you's and I need you's, and you complete my purpose and lets live forever with our legacies, ministries, and seeds joined in holy matrimonies.

Oh what a day that would be.

My spirit dances at the thought. If He will give me more than I can think or imagine, than this fusion of love must give birth to new stars, paint the origins that started, continues, and ends the universe.

It has to be given from something, some being greater than myself. See, if this was not so, than how can I bless you with my words of suffering? How and why would I freely grow you with my words of woe?

Often times I have heard let go; move on, let love die, why do you wait so long? Some of these I ask myself. But how do you stop something that started before you existed? How do you subdue something stronger than you?

How can you kill something that never dies? My answer lies…

…Not in my destination, but in my journey. So I search. I look for hidden messages in his touch, being very careful and cautious to not confuse those dialects only spoken by friends.

As an artist I have learned that you have to go with what you feel. You will either die from not doing or die trying. I feel, I want, to love. I sacrifice myself for love.

And even if this being chose never to touch me, or see me with, well, words don't always explain what things are. But if?

I will be here.

I know that I am a part of something that is plainly, bigger than I. So as I sit and wait, and wait, and wait, I take some time of this temporal realm and sing you sweet hymns of my soul's suffering while in love, yes for love.

<u>2003</u>

The Dawn of Winter

I often find myself going through the mundane routine, just to muster the energy to forget. I think I want to forget you. I make no apologies for that. This winter has lasted almost a year. I sit and watch the leaves that were once vibrant tones of green decay in caskets of frost.

It started when I realized that my love was not enough. I wanted it to warm the times and resurrect the spring. It did not. I felt my soul surrender as frost spread through the receiver.

We drifted. Two icebergs, previously one, broke.

Fuck it. Time out for the poetic language, feeding blasé bullshit, causing obesity to your ego. I want to attack. I want you to feel me. I want you to understand the hell that I have lived that is still hell, even though frozen over.

I hate that I understand why hoes trick and bitches suck dick. And niggas want to lick. All the while time just ticks and ticks on by my black ass. While on all four's I let it kick.

I don't apologize for this.

This is the first time in a long minute since I touched pen to pad.

It is, well if one wishes to place blame, I pass the buck to myself. But one may wonder why even tell you? As my friend, as my reflection, as a member who holds a piece of my soul, I need you to hear me. To know us. To see we in the eyes of each other while looking at that speck of dust that starts celestial life. These woos and woes are vital, no matter how insignificant to some or many. Even for this I do not apologize.

There are, will be, earths that call me mother and you, father.

But here I go again, wondering if you even notice, acknowledge the importance of your seed. As you let the chaos of your fucking fall on stony ground, thorny even. How long will you be hypnotized by ignorance? How long will you be comfortable in the being of "I don't knows." How long will stupidity sodomize your mental until you stand for something and shake yourself as in times pass.

Once again, I noticed that my love was not enough. Ironic even. The very thing that was pure enough, righteous enough, was not perverted enough to satisfy your appetite. I only gave you what you wanted of me, so I thought.

That was one of many deaths. I have survived though storms and blizzards that surpass my understanding. I can't show you, tell you, cry out to you of my me. My only hope is that time will echo the "what ifs" of me and you, and we, and I and blah, blah, blah.

Now, I am aloof to complex phrasing with tangible and abstract understandings, which metabolically induce endorphins, to journey to one's comprehension, promoting perceptions that make you feel good. Instead I use those that are simple:

$$1+1=2$$
$$2-1=1$$
$$2-2=0$$

Descartes proved the existence of God through math. If God is love, and love is what I am trying to give you, since everything else has failed, let us count.

One, Two
Three, Four
Too easy.

Five, Six
Seven
Eight
Hell last time you didn't even see me.

Nine
Ten
Plus one infinity.

In Spanish, Latin,
Are you close to feeling me?

4.9.2003

_____ **Viva La Resistance**

I am trying to figure out the concept of you and me.
See, I am here, supposedly in this thing with you.
But the more I seem to want you; I get categorized
as an individual that majored in four letter
superlatives.

I am more that that.

I am more than a dry construct of a reconstituted
fantasy.

I am more than a number added to the list of ghetto
contortionist.

I am more than that… So much more…so much
more to me than mediocre statements that point out

my intimated acrobatics. You know, those things
that make me hasten off the phone.

Those things that make me cop an attitude.
Those things that make me bothered, not hot.
Those things that make me wonder why I am with
you

You were right, I do think too much.

I think about my ability to be more, something, do
something life changing.
I think about my love and how it runs deep like the
river under the ocean.
I think about how I give to the point of death and
resurrection.

I think about the decrease of my self, and the
increase of someone else.
Not you, this creature that I have allowed myself to
manifest into.

But now I write my manifesto. I declare life for
someone who is destined for greatness.

I refuse to follow the steps taken by my mother.
Or will I?
Will I live in the reality that is the now, that tells me
you cannot make me happy?

This is not the world that I agreed to live in.
Will I continue to apologize for a past that I already
paid for?

Will I be tortured by the fact that if and when I say no, you will go and leave me for another who says yes?

I was never a champion of mind games.
Funny because I don't blame you.

I allow myself to get caught up in the what if's.
Like:
What if he brings me some flowers?
What if he writes me a poem?
What if he compliments my beauty, not my booty?
What if one of our conversations never mentioned
sucking dick?
What if we went outside my house this weekend?
What if he told Love?
What if his mother liked me?
What if he liked the things I do as opposed to
respecting them?
What if he really knew me?

7.4.2003

Sister...

Sista
You've been on my mind.
Oh, sista, we're two of a kind.
My sista, I'm keeping my eye on you.

I bet you think I don't know nothing,
Bout singing love's blues.
Oh sista,

94

Have I got news for you?
I've been through something.
I know you've been through your "some things"
too.

I've been up that lonely road
And I had seen a lot of shit going down.
But trust me,
No "dicked" Sirs gonna run me around.

So let me tell you something
Sista
Remember your game.
Low self esteem
Shouldn't steal your junk away.
My sister,
You shole ain't got a whole lot of time

So get your shit together
Sista
Cause honey I am doing

Fine.

2003

Poetic Haunting

Why do you choose to haunt me? Especially in
moments when I am alone and vulnerable?

I found myself doing things that remind me of my
youth. I was in an empty damp place of confusion

when I smelled the scent that belonged to you, that by the way,

Brought me back to the safety of your arms.

Intoxicated by you, I found myself stumbling across my room to grab your jacket. I hold it in both hands, bringing it to my nose, and breathe.

Immediately chills fill my body. Your scent reminds me of your hand rubbing my head.

Taking away the hurt, the agony of failures. Relieving the constipation and frustration of relational conversations gone wrong.

Taking away betrayal.
Taking away judgment.
Taking away the cancer that eats and eats and eats.

Shit, reminding me of a place when life was a safe space. And when it was truly okay to be a hippie chick.

When it was okay to cry in front of you and know that a fuck is far the fuck from me.

When love was innocent and ignorant, but fun and full of you can, you will, you are something great.

When " I love you" was said with the squint of an eye, or the gentle breeze from your sigh.

When music had color, and the wind had taste, and I heard the song of your deepest aspirations.

When loving me hurt, felt good, pissed you off,
made you cry, made you want me, hate me, miss
me, need me, love me, leave me, come back to talk
to me, to hold me, my mental, physical, spiritual.

And even now when he says something so stupid,
shit that hurts my person. Shit he thinks I should
just understand. Shit that unnecessarily breaks my
heart, even when I feel I deserve it, sometimes.

Shit that fucks my mind.
Shit that fucked my body.
Shit that fucked my soul.

Just shit.

Shit your jacket smells good.

Should I bring it to bed with me, hoping that the
magic I believe in will mystically make you appear.

Hold me…
Make it better?

Help me see the strength in me to see that I am
more than the bullshit that taunts me.

I feel bad though, because I am thinking of you
when I am with you, I mean him.

I need to hang your jacket up.

The linger of your essence is my muse.
I think about writing.

A sonnet…

A song…
A soliloquy…
A poem…
A dissertation…
A series…
A story of love.

This can get me in trouble. This is dangerous.

Maybe I should put your jacket in the back of my closet. I know you will come and one day retrieve it. But until then, I will hang it on the back of my door.

It is getting late so I will tell you more in my dreams.

2003

Freedom is not Unattainable

The first thing I see eyeing me is the lake. It always surprises me how it has the hue of not blue but green.

I look up at the clouds through the bay windows of corporate America, and I think.
In all honesty, I think that it's a damn good time to be me.

I write, say this not with an arrogant tone but to just enjoy the concept of me.

Often times I do forget that I breathe, and when my chest inflates with air, I feel the tingle of peace trickle down my spine. As I close my eyes briefly to remember the movements of the clouds, I breathe.

Then I exhale all ex-hell from my being. I push out past tortures, present insecurities, and future worries. I push out:
I cant's,
I won'ts
And
"That ain't for me's."

And I push out until my lungs feel like they are burning, but now I am discerning that I must…

…Breath.

I inhale love, peace, and patience for me. And I breathe in rest.

I rest my brow on that silver lining overhead, and I float to a place designed for my destiny.

I pass over the smog of disbelief.
I transcend those high rises built on dilapidated relationships.

And I sail in the breath of the heavens.
My dreams outline the course of my will be's.

I see that my time is now; therefore, it has been detained, and even that I am a master of.

I breathe… and I stumble upon a scent that was…oh, of a sweet savor. I thought that I have

finally reconvened with that which had made all.
But I did not.

This essence consumed my nostrils, filled my lungs,
and danced its colors through my being.

I breathe…

And breathe…

And notice that my destination is to be…

Free.

Beautifully Homeless

I see you seeing me, seeing me.
Beautiful and homeless.
Without place and or home to belong.
I see you seeing me, wishing to help.
Wondering how someone so beautiful could be me,
In this state of being.

In this state of not having a home to call my own.
Wondering how I could be wondering.
Wondering.
Just wondering how honey skin is so smooth, totally contradictory to my rags,
Shoes, bags.
Wondering how my lips are plump, while nails are filled with dirt.
Just wondering how the stench of me is not offensive.
Just wondering.
Just wondering how I hid such a pretty face under the hood.
Wondering how I've been where I have,
Going to where,
Experiencing that.
Just wondering.
I see you seeing me, seeing me.
Beautiful and homeless
Without place and or home to belong
I see you seeing me, wishing to help.
Wondering how someone so beautiful could be in this state of being.
I see you repeating those questions in your mind.
I see you.
I see new wonders pondering in your eyes about my wondering.
I see you seeing the roads of my wounds.
I see you seeing the stitches on my heart.
I see you touching the hands that touched me.
I see you in the deepest ocean of me
I see you seeing me, letting you see you seeing me.
Beautiful and homeless
Wondering if you have gotten too close to my secrets.
Wondering if you really knew.

Wondering if you really know?
Wondering if God told you?
Wondering what will I eat tonight.
Wondering where will I sleep tonight?
Wondering if you get as angry as I do.
Wondering if you woo death.
Wondering if it seduces you with sweet nothings
and promises of peace.
Just wondering. Just wondering.
Why are you beautifully homeless?
How are the homeless beautiful?
Wondering if you are without home why are you
not denied beauty?
Wondering why I am drawn to you.
Wondering why I see you seeing me.
Just pondering?
Why do your eyes pull me?
Why do you tell the stories of long ago to someone
who knows you not?
Do you love?
Do you love love?
Do you love those that love?
Has love loved to not love you in return?
I wonder, why do you share with me.
Some languages I know and some I fluently utter.
But tell me this.
How do you keep your beauty?
How does it live when there is so much that seeks to
kill it?
Attack it.
Abuse it. Shit.
How do you make it?
Is that why you're homeless?
Is your being too big that a house could not hold
you?

Were your woes to deep that no one could console
you?
Was the language complex that no one could hear?
Too much salt from your eyes to wipe that tear?
Do you get angry, so much that you give in?
I see you.
I see you seeing me.
Beautiful and homeless.
In this state of having no home to call your own.
Wondering how I could be wondering.
Wondering if that is truly a word that exists.
I see you seeing me,
Walking toward the door, so beautiful.
I wonder if she will offer a dollar, or will she ask
for one.
Just wondering.

1.11.2004

Dear You,

It is a whole new year. I have been dating
you for 12 months, but even now I feel more distant
than ever. I want to abandon this relationship. It is
too hard. I can't deal with the fact that you want to
fuck your best friend Love. I hate the fact that she
doesn't know that I am your woman. I hate that you
put me in this situation. I hate that you went to NY
and finger fucked your best friend that you are in
love with. Then you want to come home and put
your tainted hands and lips on me. How could you?

You piece of shit. I am so hurt that I am sick. I bet you are thinking that you should have fucked her after coming home to this. I don't even know if I want to be with you. I don't know if I trust you. What really gets me is that you want to fuck her, with no remorse for our relationship. You want to fuck her. She wants to fuck you. How in the hell do you think she is going to feel knowing that you placed your hands and lips all over her body while dating me? You put me back to the incident with Shaun and Dominique. Whether you wish to admit it or not, I am second. You were willing to break up with me to be with her for one night. She has your loyalty and your heart. You love her traits, mannerisms, body, past, everything. She is your mirror. Not me. The only reason why you are with me instead of her is because I am in Chicago. I am your girlfriend by proximity. My stomach hurts because I am in love with you and hurt all at the same time. I didn't want to live like this. I don't want to love again. It is too painful. I don't want to make love anymore. I don't want this anymore. I have become pathetic and I don't want this anymore. I am too different. I can't give myself to you. I make love to you, sex you, and fuck you because I think my body is sacred. So I share it only with you. But you don't have that belief, causing me to think that I am wasting my time. Oh yeah, by the way. You are not a piece of shit. I just wish that I didn't feel like I am loving you more than you do me. My heart hurts, real bad. I can't stop crying. I hate that I love you so much that I act like a schoolgirl, writing a Dear John letter with tears all over the place. Parts of me need you. But parts of me can't deal with you. I am starting to not respect you. And before I hate you, become numb and not care, or fuck my best friend out of retaliation, I will leave you. I can't share you as easily as you are willing to share me. I have never been that type of woman and I am not going to start. I'd like to think that when you gave yourself to me it was because of the same reasons I gave mine, but it wasn't. You could have been thinking about fucking Love while you were fucking me. I want you to tell her about us. I want you to risk everything. You said you can't help how I feel; well, this will make me feel better. But you won't, will you? I know you don't want to lose her. Instead you are willing to lose me.

I cannot, will not be your woman. I am no longer your girlfriend. Call me selfish if you want, but you have been selfish with this situation for far too long. I cannot be your girlfriend while you want to fuck your best friend, who also wants you, who also doesn't know about us. It's like living a double life. How am I supposed to know that you are not doing other shit? I don't know if you are loyal to me. That's why it is so easy for you to think that I am going to fuck him, because you have it in your mind that you are going to fuck Love. I can't deal with this. I tried to explain this to you, how much it affected me, but you chose to leave it the way it is, you don't want Love knowing about us. How can I love you as your woman with this on my heart? How can I trust you knowing that you would have fucked if I didn't make you promise not too? How can I respect this relationship when I know you were going to dump me to spend the weekend with her? How can I give my body to you -something I believe is sacred- when you give your's so freely to whoever you deem worthy? How can I continue to respect you after all of this mental anguish? I wanted to be with you. I wanted to continue being your girlfriend even after you looked me in the eyes and told me you wanted to fuck your best friend. I wanted to stay even after you told me you were going to make her burst because that is the least you can do, because it would be a waste not to, after driving all the way to NY. I wanted to stay even after you told me you kissed her, fingered her, and more likely than not rubbed, kissed, fondled her body, while telling her all the things she wanted to hear. I imagine you guys talking, and she asked you if you were seeing someone, and you reply no, no one special. God my heart, my heart hurts. My heart is broken and I never wanted to be hurt again. So I bid you farewell. I am still your friend, but your love, as a boyfriend is no longer needed. Or welcome.

I
kept
others close by
taking care of them.
I am a HYPER HELPER.

Hey Babes,

I just wanted to write to you to tell you all the things you already know. So I guess in my own way, this is my love letter to you. I know this might be gushy but I really care for you. It is weird for me to write this. I always think in the back of my mind that I shouldn't do stuff like this. Maybe the timing would be off? Or maybe I am sitting over here all happy with glee while you are trying to figure out a way on how to cope? Any who, I just want to say that I appreciate you. You are the most important person in my life. I thank you for being a big support system. I know that it is not easy being with me and that I drive you crazy sometimes, but I just needed to let you know that you mean the world to me. You have seen me at my lowest point in life and you stayed around. Even when you wanted to run away you came back. Through all the depression and complaining about my weight, you were there. When I wanted to just give up on everything, you were there. I thank you. You have been very kind even when you didn't want to be. You have loved me through thick and thin. I don't know where I would be if it wasn't for your constant encouragement. And now look at me. I am thinner. I am working a job I actually look forward to going to. I am Happy. And I am in love. Who would have known?

Love,

Starr

Mother

To you, my mother.
To you, my mother. I wish all the best.
To you, my mother I would give the world.
To you.
For you, my mother. My eyes swell with water that
wants to come out, but pride dries.
For you.

For you, my mother. The first woman I ever loved,
even before seeing myself as one.
Modeling myself as you. Walking in your 7 and a
half sized shoe until my feet got too big.
Walking, hurting in shoes too small.

But if I can't fit them shoes I can at least have as
many.

I danced in my glorified isms of ghetto wealth. Who
knew they made fuchsia gators in size eleven?

I don't know.
Why we are more like associates than friends.
More like distant lovers that ended on a bad note.
More like everything other that what we're
supposed to be.

I don't know.

I don't know why I take a deep breath when you
call. I don't know why I am nervous to see you. I
don't know why a year seems too short.

I know I love you.
I know my heart hurts.

I know I cry because I am not best friends with my
Ma, and don't want to be.

Maybe?
Maybe. I need you.
Maybe. My soul needs you.
Maybe. A part of me thinks you are crazy.
Maybe. I share your demons.

I look in the mirror and I see you. I see Deddy too.

I see you both talking to me. Wishing me well and
the best.

Do you know that sometimes I don't want to be
strong? I don't want to be the one people turn to.
I hate that I have to plan what to say to you. This
should be easy right. Right?

So what is the problem? What is truly the issue?

Honestly. I do think, can think of some times that
occurred in my life where I have felt
    Abandoned
        Betrayed
            Neglected
                Hurt
                    By you.

But I know you probably feel the same about me.
Maybe. There was some mis-communication.
Maybe. It is too late to make up for childhood
dramas. But if this is false. Then:
            Why am I obsessed?
            Why do I care what people
think?

Why do I care how I look?
Why do I feel good about
myself only when I help others?
Why do I feel guilty if I say
"no?"
Why do I feel like I owe you
something?

Why do I cry alone?
Why do I make jokes when I
hurt?
Why do I feel too dirty for
God?
Why do my friends call,
come by only when they
need, they want, or, I would
be good for some fucking
committee that don't give a
shit if you need help? Or if
they need to feel affirmed?
Why do I cry quietly?
Why was I molested?
Why was I raped?
Why has no one had the
courage to do something?
Why I have to deal with this
all-alone 15, 20 years later?
Why did my baby die?
Why did I fall head over hills
for a gay man?
Why did pastor feel he could
touch me like that?
Why did cancer take my
father?
Is that how I'm going to die?
Feeble, frail, alone?

Is that why I have gained so much weight?

How come I don't want a real job but want all the benefits?

Why didn't I believe him when he told me I was beautiful?

Why did I die a little when he told me he did crack?

Why did I sleep with her only to prove I really liked him?

Why do I want stuff to feel accomplished?

Why did it take me so long to write this?

Why do I collect things I know I

Don't need,
Won't use,
Was
on sale?

Who am I proving my existence too?

Who other than Christ needs to affirm my validity?

Why did it take me so long to write this? This is the true letter. Not that casual conversation that came back in the mail. This.

This is a reflection of me.
This window to my soul disguised in a corn silk colored suit.

You know. I was thinking about uncle Craig's. I thought about how he was the darkest out of all of

you. June Bug is what Grandma called him. I
remember him telling me that the chicken will tell
you when it needed to be flipped. Because the
grease will get real quiet. You just gotta listen.

I think about him telling me, that. In the moldy
basement that I loved to smell.

"You just got to listen."

> Cause we all know about times when you real
> hungry
> And
> You ain't ate all day
> And
> You so happy that you don't have to cook because
> you are real tired.
> and
> You bite into and the most juiciest piece of fried
> chicken on the planet to
> only look down and see that all that juice was
> well....

No need to get gross.

You just gotta listen.

I listen to the prayers over-shadowed by cries of
sorrow when that car came and took Unk away to
the other side.

I listened to Grandpa's blues medley on the guitar.

I listened to uncle Peter Rabbit drink his brew of get
right instead of MGD.

And I listened to you.

I listened to you cry for brighter days and warmer
nights.

I listened to your tears of pain when Deddy didn't
touch you quite right.

I listened to you love a man that love you and him.

I listened.
I listened to your longing for someone to love, love
you, to love us.

I listened to your prayers for

                          No more Spam nights
                          No more no-good
niggas
                          No more so-called
friends
                          Get my baby off
drugs
                          Make my baby
smarter
                          Make my baby love
me
                          No more roaches
                          No more rats.
                          No more guns
                          No more drugs

With promises to…

                          Pay more tithes
                          Be a good church
usher
                          No more stripping

Be a good mother

I listened.

You just gotta listen.

I listen to Grandma and how she had you at 14.
How you had Parnel at 16. I listen to how she made
you feel.

I bet you could write this letter too huh.

Lord knows I have fallen short.

I listen to this letter in my head.
     And I hear.
         I hear.
              A lot of people speaking at
              once. But only when it comes
              to certain topics. Like in the
              cinema of me, I feature
              productions like:
              "My daughter the Bitch"
              "Homeless Man Man"
              "Ron vs. Mari- favorite vs.
         Black Sheep"

But some people walk out. Tired.
Tired of those movies.

Down the street the feature presentation is "What
if?"

Everyone goes to see that.

Who hurt you Ma?

Who did it?
Who gave you your isms of ghetto wealth?
Who told you that love started between your legs
and not between your ears?
Who painted the picture of white picket fences with
2.5 kids, husband, car and a cat?
Who told you that tough love meant extension
cords, shoes and pipes?
Who embarrassed you at church?
Who did you fall in love with at a young age?
Who told you it was wrong?

     Hell bound?

     Sinful?

Who was the person that told you that the only
dancers that are important or make money are those
that threw their clothes off?
Who told you that the way you moved wasn't art?
I just want to know because...
Because those things are far from the truth.

Someone has played too cruel of a joke on us, and
well.
        THE SHIT WASN'T FUNNY!

I don't know who gave it to you, to give to me, but I
am not taking it.

        INSTEAD

Instead.

I will take the knowledge of taking whatever you have in the cabinet. Throwing it together to make a miracle meal.

I will take my $.85 super transfer and follow my mother across the city of Chicago.

I will take the pride in your eyes when you saw me:
       Write my first book,
       Sing my first song on stage,
       Recite my first poem,
       Act in my first play,
       Dress for prom,
       Graduate from high school
       And college
       Get my first apartment.

I will take the laughs we had when I told you your feet stink.

I will take the prayers for me to be better, live better than you could have ever imagined.

I will listened to the stories from my sister about how you wanted me. Your baby girl.

I will listen to this song when it plays for me, for my own seed.

I will listen beyond the hurt to hear the "I love you and I need you's".

To you, my mother I would give the world to.

For you, my mother. My eyes swell with water that wants to come out but pride dries.

For you.

For you, my mother. The first woman I ever loved, even before seeing myself as one.

Walking, hurting in shoes too small.

But if I can't fit them shoes, I can at least have as many.

Wed May 4 12:49:58 2005

Today.

Today I feel like writing. Writing something that tells a little bit more about me. Something that inspires me to face the day and tells me that I can make it. Something to encourage me as in times passed. Something. Something to feed to the nations to declare to them, those who process in the masses as sole individuals that they are not alone. There is a comfort in knowing that. There is a sense of relief just by knowing. A power, if you will.

     I have been singing. I have been happy. But the strangest thing has happened. Actually two strange things have happened. The first is that I realized that I am still in love with Eliot. This is crazy, I know. How did this happen? I thought that my love for him died that long night at the Murphy's. That was a horrible night. I felt as if my heart was stabbed with a jagged knife and yanked out of my chest. That was the night I gave up. The night I gave in to defeat. And yet, I survived. I survived starvation, neglect and ridicule. I can't believe it. I forced myself to hate him. Remember the hurtful things he did to me? I still feel. I just knew that I did not, was not, in love with him when we slept together that night. I did not feel the sting of needing him. But I started singing. I was singing and I saw him. I saw him up there directing. And for the most insane moment in my life, I loved him. He was beautiful. He was well. His eyes shined and his soul was renewed. He loved. His voice ran through the room like an escaped prisoner with no consequences. His voice danced with the freedom of life. And I fell in love. All of a sudden, nothing mattered. All of a sudden, I knew where I was supposed to be. It felt right. And I haven't felt right in a long time. Then he looked at me. It was with the warmth of familiarity, yet the newness of a first kiss. We saw each other. Feeble, frail, wanting, longing for this moment in time to sing. To sing a self-song. To feel the words with the experience of life. To express to the world how a perfect being can be used through imperfection. And it felt good. I felt like I was home. I felt safe. I felt pretty. I was light. I was singing.

Orlando is an ambitious man. I do adore him. I missed him. I usually see him, and he I. But I guess turning twenty-seven and being a sophomore in college can be challenging. I really love him, but sometimes he makes me cry. Like I said, he is an ambitious man. He is a productive visionary. He sees. He does. He moves. He finishes. I try to understand. Don't get me wrong. I am no stranger to hard work. I am a stranger to love. This is what I have with this man. Love. I do understand why he gets so angry sometimes. He is focused. He has to be. He has exasperated every other option; therefore, school is his only road to success. He is a smart man, too. Even I quiver under him with my brilliant intelligence and high IQ. But at times I find him tortured. His soul is so wounded. I thought that it could have been the stresses of serving during 9/11. I thought it could have been the insecurities of being older while in undergrad. I now see that this stems from a much older place in time. While growing up, Orlando had a twinkle in his eyes. He had a spark of joy that was so ingrained in him, it was a second skin. He loved life. He wrote about it. Drew it. Sung sweet soliloquies about it. Danced to it's rhythms. Then something happened. He was a victim of church corruption. Our pastor, growing up, was more focused on the panting of people's panties than the prosperity of people's souls. See all the while we were growing up with the Word of God, Pastor was sowing seeds of discourse, adultery, you know all those things that he taught Orlando and I as youths to be sin. That's a damn shame. I was fortunate. After my brief exposure to molestation by my pastor, I left. But Orlando, even though he was not there physically he was still tied to a man that he wanted to release. His mother still goes. So now, in his adult life he has abandoned the church. He believes that it is full of needy people begging to God about problems that they have already been equipped to solve. I do agree to an extant with this, but what really bothers me is his bitterness that is merged with this truth. I believe he feels that these people are weak. If he confesses to be a part of such a society, than he himself would be weak. And maybe, just maybe be a contributor to the promotion of lying, adulteress clergymen. All the while, something inside him has died. He thinks that he has gotten stronger, but he is weakened. His zeal for life and all its wonders has died. His ambition is rooted in the belief that God has equipped him to be success; therefore, that is his life's journey. But he loves me. The object of his affection is the door to fear. I am his evil seed that reminds him that there is more to life than just money, and in turn he hates me. He doesn't understand why I call him just to tell him that I missed him. He sees it as offensive. I was inconsiderate to want to see him at 8pm, when he needed to be at work by 9:45pm. I was selfish. I missed him. I haven't seen him since I started singing.

So here I am. Here I am. Trying. I am trying. I don't wish to write of sorrows. I don't want to sing those sad songs of mistreatment by the one I love.

I went to class last night. I have to say that I was not too fond of these particular ladies. I felt that they lacked ambition. I was wrong. They want. They hope to be happy, be that with school, money, life, and love. They just want to be happy. That is what I took with me as I eavesdropped on a very loud discussion in class. Tessa is 21 with three children. Her oldest is 6. The father of the younger two has taken control of her. He has her car. Her mind. Her soul. To make a very long (yet entertaining) story short, she was unhappy. Pansy - a former stupid woman- beseeched her to let go, let God, and wake up. Needless to say, her words were just what I needed after getting off the phone with Orlando at 8:05pm.

So this past week was hard. I hurt my ankle.
The very same ankle that I sprained a couple of years ago. I had missed a week of hair school, and to top it all off, I lost my $300 cell phone. I just wanted to cool out. I got in from work on Friday. While having the biggest BF (bitch fit) that I could have, my sister told me that Eliot called. I called him back. He wanted to know if I was busy. I told him no, due to my fabulous day. He was glad because he wanted to go out, and he wanted me to go with him. So I did.

He came and picked me up from my house. I was not quite ready so he just hung out with my sister and I. I was so pretty. I had on some tight, hip hugging jeans with a lime green sleeveless top. He immediately told me how hot I looked. I was feeling so much better all ready.

We arrived at the club. He held my hand, guiding me threw a parade of gay men. Some how it just didn't matter. I was with Eliot. He took me to the bar. Asked me what I would like. I told him to

124

surprise me like he always does. He spent $35 on drinks. I told him jokingly; "I guess I have to give you some tonight huh." He said, "we'll see."

We found some leather couches to sit on. The ambience was very appealing. Since we were both tipsy, we were making jokes on how the environment reminded us of the Wiz. *"You got to be seen green, wouldn't be caught dead in red."* Then the conversation started getting serious, real. I don't even know who started it. I will take the blame. I probably said something like I missed you, or I am so glad you hooked up with me. All I remember are the really good parts. Oh, I remember. He asked if I felt uncomfortable when he took my top off last week (We tend to fool around sometimes.). I was like "oh God, no. It was fine." I went on to tell him how great it was how he helped me to reach my climax. I get chills just thinking about it. He told me how he had a great time, too. He went on to express how we could improve our next threesome with elaborate positions. I was impressed. Not because I was wowed by this great lover of mine, but by the fact that this lover was a gay man. And I am a heterosexual woman. All I could tell myself was that he loved me. He later told me how important I was in his life. Then he states how he wants a baby. I made a joke "you know I got you in a couple of years." He asked me "but what about Orlando?" I told him that we already discussed it. I love you both. He asked, "but how does he really feel about you wanting to have a kid with a gay man? Because people say one thing and feel another." This was something for me to think about. I just held his hand and told him that I loved him. I loved him before there was any physical. I loved him before I saw his talents and after I saw his faults. "I love you for you." He told me that he loved me too. He apologized for not being around. I told him that I knew that he would always come back. He went on to say that I was going to be one of his friends for life. I asked him if I made him uncomfortable with the newness of our sexual attraction toward each other. He expressed that it was at first. He goes on to say "I didn't know how to react because, in the past, I know that you had feelings for me like I did for you, but we were friends and I didn't want to mess that up, so I kept my distance...." He kept talking, but my mind was stuck on him stating that he had feelings for me. I have waited a long time for him to tell me that. I was in love with this man. There were long nights that I would sit up and just wonder if he felt the same for me as I did him. And how in love we would be. And how great the world would turn out because we would have given birth to our love. And now I hear it. After a part of me died. After I let him go. After I give my heart to another. After. Parts of me were flattered. Parts of me were angry. I could have saved a lot of time from dwelling in the limbo of what if, if only he had told me sooner. But everything works together for the good of them that love the Lord. So I just finished listening.

A juke song came on the monitor. He was giving me the most tantalizing lap dance ever conceived. I even reached in my wallet and pulled out some singles. I later informed him that the money was my contribution to the gas fund. He laughed. I laughed. I told him to remember that we are in a gay bar.

Taylor was running late again. As usual. Eliot calls him to see where he was. He was somewhere doing something. At the same time Eliot and I looked out the window and see Taylor walking down the street with his entourage of gay comrades. Gay men are so funny. Eliot and I continue to talk. I can barely stand. Eliot always gets me great drinks. I had to go pee. Walking to the restroom was like walking down the runway in stilettos, very difficult. While doing my business, I can't help but to think back on the conversation. I was telling myself to blow it off. All the while angry because this information has come too late. I can't do anything about it now. There is a knock on the latrine door. It is my knight in shining armor. "Hey we're going to go meet Taylor." He grabs my hand and leads me through the crowd. All I see is his long locks moving from side to side. They were wooing me.

Taylor has a group of unknowns with him. So it is my policy to harass people. It is my formal icebreaker. I see one of the guys I met three weeks ago. He had some smoke. I followed him. I smoked. I found Eliot. We went to the other club. While in line, Taylor confesses that he does not have money to get in. Eliot snaps. "Not only did you have us waiting for you and your dumb ass friends for two hours, you mean to tell me that you do not have money to get in? You knew where we were going...." Taylor walks away. I grab Eliot and proceed into the club. He was so pissed. I walked him to the bar. All the while he is pissed and ranting. I told him to get us some drinks. I handed him some cash. We get our drinks and proceed to the sitting area. All of a sudden, this guy knocks over Eliot's drink. I didn't want this to be the last straw so I gave him mine. I was still buzzing anyway. The place we were sitting reminded me of the seating arrangement in a sauna. I sat on the risers and he stood by my legs. The music was nice. The club reminded me of a scene from Queer as Folk. I saw men standing on risers dancing like the gay Coyote Ugly. I didn't care. I was with Eliot.

So I'm grooving to the music and he ask me a question. "Can I have a no consequence, no repercussion kiss?" Sure, why not. I kid you not. As our lips touched, time froze. Our rhythm was like dancing to a mellow hip-hop song. Just right. Everyone had suddenly disappeared. I felt his heart beat a song that only sang in his kiss. I forgot where I was as I caressed his face, bringing him closer to me. His lips were so soft. Damn. I could go on. But the people were slowly coming back. And the music got louder and faster. I hope he didn't notice that I was stunned for a minute. I shook myself, you know, like nothing happened. He leaned over and whispered in my ear, "You so nasty." Well what can I say? Once again I had to remind him that we were in a gay club. I hate him so much.

The rest of the night was filled with innocent flirting and touching. We went to grab some cheap food. Went back to my place. Smoked some smoke. And laughed. I ended up lying on his thigh. I passed the hell out. I don't even know how I got into my bed, or my bedclothes. I later recapped with Orlando the great time I had. Orlando is not a jealous man, plus he was and is my friend as well as my lover. He was so happy that I got out. He is not the going out type. But he does enjoy restaurants. So Orlando and I went to the Golden Nugget. We had such a great time. We laughed like old times. Life was good again and it was good to be me. I can't help but think, though, how I have two men that I love, one gay and the other focused on his pursuit of happiness, and both of them love me. Yet neither one wants to be with me. Well, at least not right know. My life is so complicated. But it is my life. And I don't regret it at all. Not even the loss of my phone.

Tue Jun 21 11:02:58 2005

Dear You,

Here I am writing to keep my sanity. I am writing words of feelings that are spawned because I don't know you. I don't know me. I feel nauseous because it dawned on me that I might have allowed you to use me. I have lost my mind, my self worth. All this just by letting you in my life. I have become the lesser version of me and I am sick. I am sick of it. I don't totally blame you. I down played my glory for something that I could see, and feel for the right now. I am a shamed of who I have become. Parts of me hate you. And other parts of me are glad that you came into my life. You allowed me to see that love is something more. Something that I forgot. I remember when I asked you if you were in love with me. And you shrugged your shoulders as if I playfully made some satire. But I knew right there and then your answer. You may not want to say it to spare my feelings, but I know the truth. That truth has made me free. It has nothing to do with anyone else. This is what I want. I want to be free. I want to wake up and not dread our interaction. I want to have a conversation, and hope that this will be the time that you snap on me, so that I can leave. I want our so-called sex to end. Because it is not good anymore. It used to be a time were you wanted to make love to me and now you barely want to fuck me. I have decided that you are playing games that I don't have time for. Life is too short. I realized why it didn't work out before. I realized why our baby had to die. And I realize why we could not, cannot, be anything more than friends. Thank you for helping me realize that. I am not even mad. I am just glad that our time was not wasted. I am grateful for the gift that you have given me, the gift of the truth. The gift of freedom. The painful gift that only a true friend could give. A gift of love.

Deddy transcended.
But as far as I can tell.
I still have to live.

Aug 30 12:37:36 2005

Mission Complete

So I have to tell you about this dream I had last night. *I remember being at an open mic. I performed this poetry/free style. I was really nervous and thought less of myself, but it was actually very good. People came up to me and everything. Then it was time for Eliot to get up and sing with this group. They did very well. It was so good that it turned to worship. Everyone on the stage was just gone. It put this song in my head. I started singing it. It started coming alive. It followed me through the rest of my dream. I remember singing it as loudly as I can to/through the sky to God. I kept hearing in my mind to give it to Eliot.*

*In the dream I met some people that tried to
make me forget the song.*

*A guy with a knife wearing a red baseball cap.
He tried to scare me. At first I was, but then
I turn around to face him. I noticed that
there was a butter knife in my hand. I also
noticed that there was a thin silver fence
between us. So I stabbed him through the hole
in the fence. I told him to stop trying to
distract me. I have to make it to the end of
the dream. He walked with me to the fat man.*

*A fat man with a pale blue, tight t-shirt. He
just leaned up against the gate talking. He
looked like he had just got through eating. We
were in a field. He wanted me to sing. So I
was singing the song. He wanted to change it.
So I got down in the grass and I sung it
straight to the sky as loud as I could. Till
the ground shook. I got up and grabbed his
mouth and told him to stop trying to distract
me. I turned around and I was on the second
floor balcony of a brown stone building. Think
of Romeo and Juliet, but the only thing I saw
surrounding me were other buildings. Like the
back entrance into an apartment complex.*

*A tall beautiful girl with long, brown hair,
who I called a witch, threw an old fashioned
bike at me. I told her that I was going to
deliver the song. She was talking to me. All
apologetic now. Like she was my friend.
Insuring me of her good intent. I said, "If
you not a witch than why are you levitating."
"I got to wake up." I began to slap myself in
the dream.* I woke up.

Song:
*I need you.
I need you.
Teach me how
to be
completely*

Free to.

Free with you.
I need to be free with you.
Teach me how
to be
completely
Free to.

I have seen so many things. Those
Things have tried to turn my eye. Those
Things have made me run away.
And made you weep, utterly cry.
But then I felt your pain inside
And all I wanted to do was die. So I
Don't know what to do.
All I ask is teach me how to be
Free to.

I need you
Teach me how
to be
completely
Free to

"Sorry it took me so long to respond. There was a lot in the dream. I think that the dream was for you and Eliot. You are a woman of words and there is always a message in your mouth; whether it is through poetry or a prophetic utterance, etc. and the enemy has always tried to distract you; but look at your strength and your boldness in the dream. The only thing I have to say in regard to that is you had a butter knife, which is a dull instrument. YOU should have had a two-edged sword - the word. But you overcame the distractions; it showed that you were focused and could not be moved - that's good. The guy with the red cap and the knife was a spirit of fear.

The fat guy in the pale blue shirt - pale blue represents the
flesh - notice this - he wanted you to change your song. If you
had changed it, you probably would have forgotten the song
when you woke up. This guy represented the music industry of
the world (notice he was the only one that asked you to sing) -
he represented a gluttonous spirit and a spirit of greed. Notice
you sang until the ground shook, which represents the freedom
that will come to Eliot from singing this song - it reminds me
of Paul in Prison. He was in chains and he praised and
worshipped God all night until the ground shook and the
prison doors flew open. The enemy has tried to change Eliot 's
song. But if he sings this song and refuses to change it, the
ground will shake and all chains will be broken.

The witch - two things about her. You may have encountered
a spirit that has been working against Eliot. I say this because
you felt it necessary to tell her that you were going to deliver
the song. You can also call her a principality or power of the
air - the other demons was working under her; she was the
"stronghold." All the other demons could do was try to scare
you and suggest that you change the song. She actually threw
a tangible object at you. She was the root of the distractions.
She was the one orchestrating the attacks against you in the
dream. Her throwing the bike at you - riding a bike in the
spirit, sometimes, means you working through your flesh - her
throwing the bike at you was her throwing your past at you
and/or presenting you with the option of getting on and taking

yourself out of the covenant with God. But you refused, again you overcame them. Her talking to you and insuring her intent was deception and confusion.

Notice you were in the field and then you went to a brownstone building surrounded by apartments. You are blessed in the city and blessed in the field; and God is with you wherever you go.

I believe that song is a confession for the both of you. That song will get Eliot to the place where he can sing and change the atmosphere into one of worship like he was designed to do. And if you continue to sing that song, you'll notice a change that will manifest naturally.

What did you get from the dream?"

Wow. That was for real. To be honest, I just knew what I had to do. I really didn't get anything until after I wrote it down. I remember waking up and saying to myself that I don't deserve this song. Orlando had spent the night, too. We didn't do anything but I just felt that I am not in a place to receive something that was so pretty and strong. I have been singing it all day to keep the melody in my head and when I want to do something else, I get sleepy. Only singing the song has kept me awake. Also, as I was singing it over and over it got better and better. It was so funny because I told God that I am not the singer, just a lowly messenger. My voice even sounds better. Jesus, huh? Oh yeah. As I sing, I see beads of water. Like

water dripping from icicles or dew on leaves. And I texted
Eliot as soon as I got to work and told him to call me on my
lunch, so I could sing it to him. I emailed him, too.

"Cool. And you receiving the song in the place that you are in
is just the grace and mercy of our Father. The question is,
now that you have it, what are you going to do with it? Don't
let it fall to the ground."

Fri Sep 16 11:39:31 2005

Preghi

Thank you for whomever will get this. I appreciate you taking
time to come to someone's aid in prayer. I have not been to
AFC in about a year. I miss you guys. I have gone through
some very hard things, from fornication to depression, from
contemplating suicide to abuse of alcohol. My heart is
saddened because I am still hurting from my father's death last
year from cancer. I am only 26 and it is really hard. I pretty
much had to take care of everything when all I wanted was
someone to take care of me. And now with nothing to do, I
feel empty. I have lost my dance. I know God is still with me
but I feel like no one understands. I apologize for this being so
long, but this is my truth. I feel like God's people have
abandoned me. Everyone loved me when I was "righteous,"
but now that I have fallen, now that I need, no one cares. I
have grown angry and bitter. My life is at a stand still. I thank

137

God everyday for His mercy and grace, but I know that I am living a mediocre life. I don't know what this letter can do, but I don't just send this out for myself but for my friends Orlando and Eliot, who at some point in their lives felt hurt, rejection and abandonment as well. Thank you family for reading and praying.

Hey Dear,
How are you and the girls? I just wanted to drop you a line to check in and let you know that I am still alive and stuff. Sorry it has been so long for me to contact you guys. So, what's new? Life is pretty much the same over here, except now I don't care if people don't understand my randomness. Well, hear from you soon.

Love,

Starr

Angry Fan Mail

I am understanding the concept of being indifferent.

My rent. My gas. My lights.
Those tears only heard by God. In deep dark
silence.
And so I sit indifferent.
Upset with the fact that I am just one. Just one
stopping and staring.
Getting fat off Fritos.
Watching you pound on those doors. I am
ashamed.
Ashamed right now to be American.
Ashamed that I went outside with unshaven Bush.
I beseech the forgiveness of God for being
indifferent.
Being so caught up in my own mess.
Garbage.
Being not responsible for those things that I have
paraded.
Applauding my blackness like "pink" being what's
new and hot.
Fashionable, unrealistic to those things that needed
to be said.
Upset because that is the only way to feel.
Feeling left.
Feeling abandoned.
Remembering when Spam was a delicacy.
Remembering when lights were a luxury.
Remembering prayers to God to hold the snow
because that garbage can don't make good wet.
Just remembering.

Feeling angry with myself because like others I
wanted to place blame.
I want to fuss and bitch about coulda, shoulda.
All the time ordering extra mild sauce.
Damn
I thought I was an individual.
I got so caught up in my own understanding of
isms.
I'm just a wounded leader trying to lead.
But I bow down and follow lead.
I didn't mean to be indifferent.
Paralyzed by my privilege. Trapped by my guilt.
Clouded with my own vanity.
But I remember…
… My mama out there shaking her ass to make ends
meet.
… Wearing hats to bed as roach repellant.
… Sleeping on the floor and being grateful.
… Praying for better days.
I am angry because I forgot.
I let my degrees bow me to my knees and renounce
you.
Never knew what it felt like to have white guilt.
I know the TV is turned off.
And only three more years of purgatory, but forgive
me.
I remember when Auntie Rose had a can of corn,
and Poochie had the peas.
With mama, potatoes.
With you, canned beef.
Produced the biggest pot of stew for all of us to eat.
We had leftovers, 3 fish and 5 loaves miracles.
Water to pennies, miracles.
Brought back from the dead, miracles.
Understanding, choosing, knowing, believing, doing
and achieving "feeling safe" miracles.

Only indifferent about the proposed impossibilities.
Sincerely.

Wed Nov 30 17:05:03 2005

I.C.U.

I am sick with love.
I have done the unthinkable; I am obsessed with the
need to be loved. To the point that I want to puke.
My stomach rumbles as if I must shit myself.
Just thinking of you.
And you.
I am so upset with the fact that I cannot choose, or that
fact that I even have to.
I feel that death is upon me, and even so that would be
easier than to live with the fact that I may not have
either one of you as my own.
So I cower by just loving you both.
I was fine until I caught a case of the hates.
I was cool until I realized I was getting older and all
those that gave me wisdom met God.
I was cool until I realized I was all alone. Felt alone.
But knew that God was there. Is there.
Not to be a sick bastard, but God can and can't give
me what I crave.
I am a heathen.
I feel too much. I feel sick. I smell sick.
I thought someone walked pass me with the foul smell
of a weakened soul only to notice I was alone and
have been.
I am sick.
I taste my flesh's pain to love. So much that it grows
ill.
And Haunted.
Forever haunted by the fact that he loves me, but can't

141

touch me.

And that he loves me now but can't see loving me later.

So I hope to conceive by a man that loves his own and marry a man who despises all that makes me me.

I am sick.

Of trying to justify a way to persuade myself that this is best.

What will I do when my children ask me why daddy lives with a man?

What will I do when my husband feels abused from supporting a family he did not create, want?

I am sick.

My heart is torn and I want to die.

My life is shit and I run in circles.

Where is he?

The guy that will love me like he, and I and I will be like the most High. HAPPY.

Where are you?

I pray for better days with warm suns and cool nights to cuddle in.

I silently scream your name. Not knowing what it is.

Why won't you come to me? What have I done to make you hide your face from me?

Have I shamed you by my split heart?

Have I hurt you?

Do I know you?

Am I blinded by what I think I want instead of seeing who you truly are?

My deepest fear is that he is right in front of my face.

I fear that he sees my sickness and runs away confused.

I fear he smells my soul and regurgitated.

I fear he does not exist.

I used to believe in happily ever after. I used to believe in true love.

I used to believe.

Maybe I am thinking too much?

Maybe he got away?
Maybe he was that guy in high school that I laughed at?
Maybe he was the one I though I was too good for?
Maybe it is just not my time?
I feel sick.
If I have to throw up the office trash can will be my comfort.
The melodic blend of words will be my children running to my rescue.
My God will be my lover to wipe away my tears and tell me it will be okay.
I keep coughing uncontrollably.
The tears keep falling.
I miss grandma.
I miss you Deddy.
I know if you were here you would tell me the truth about myself.
You would not honey glaze anything to spare my frosted-covered feelings.
You would be my example of a man.
You would remind me what love is.
I know I got my brothers but they are not quite you, just your reflection.
I hate that I put so much...
I hate that I weigh so much on...
Words leave me and...
I cry...
Rivers, seas, oceans to feel family.
To understand my place on this pool table.
I know you come to me in my dreams and I was afraid. I was sad.
But believe it or not I am better.
Who knew that...
Maybe I...
All this is about you, you.
You were the first man that I ever loved.
You were the one that made me feel special.

It has nothing to do with them I know that now.
I miss you Abraham.
I'll be loving you always.
My lion, my Aslan.
Here goes the therapy.
Damn, I didn't mean for her to see my crying. Now
she is going to ask me if I need a break or something.
Anything the devil can do to try and stop progress, she
will. The bastard.

Deep down, I feel that I need to be married and start a
family because you are gone.
Deep down, I feel that I want to be with Eliot because
he wants kids, he is an artist, he likes to go out and
have fun. I can talk to him. I see me spending the rest
of my life with him, but he loves men. I could not bare
to tell you when you were alive because I didn't know
what you would say. I thought that it seemed naive
and foolish.
Deep down, I want to be with Orlando at times. We
have really good moments together. He has a great
ear. He is not afraid to speak the truth no matter what.
He actually reminds me a lot of you with his
meekness and honesty, but neither he nor his family
really accepts me. I always feel like I have to prove
myself around them. Don't get me wrong; I love them.
I grew up with them. But I am that little girl trying to
get their approval. I hate that.

So here I am.
Should I find someone else?
Should I continue to feed my addiction through the
both of them?
Should I just leave them both alone and focus on me?
Should I just choose?
Should I just wait?
My being says that there is an urgency because I feel
sick.

I don't know what is wrong with me and I am so far from God.

Honestly I feel that my time is near and I have accomplished nothing.

I wonder...
What will they say when...
Who will say to me I was loved and loved..?

Kid Talk

Dear You,
I've been needing to tell you this for some time. I will try to keep this as short as possible. I want to have children one day. But most importantly, I want to have a family. I have always imagined that I will have kids by the man of my dreams, who not only loved me, but also wanted to be with me. I fear that this may not be the case with you. The funny thing is that you are the man of my dreams. You are the one I can see spending the rest of my life with. But I just don't know if you want me in that equation. I know you love me and want me, and picture me being the mother of your children. But I don't know if you see me as your wife. I just don't know and that is something I need to know. I don't want to be like my parents. I need to feel like I will be giving my kids a fighting future. And in my mind that means two parents that show love to each other and them in one house. Maybe this is far fetched. And maybe I am just dreaming of a fairy tale life, but that is my image of a family. That is my image. That is what I want. I feel that I have to share this with you now before we decide to do something that we will regret in the future. I needed to let you know where I was coming from. Don't get me wrong, I do love you. But I don't want to place unfair

145

expectations on you without discussion. I don't want to walk into parenting alone or end up hating you. I don't want to have kids thinking that it will win your love for me either. I just want it to be right. I want to at least try. But unfortunately if I can't have this with you, I will have to wait until I can. I will have to wait for someone who is willing to be that and do that with me. I am so sorry. I cherish your friendship deeply and I hope that nothing changes that. I can offer nothing but the truth. Whatever your response will be, I will understand.

-T

Thu Nov 3 15:50:50 2005

Constantly

Constantly telling myself.
Constantly saying
That I can't fall for you.

Constantly wooing
And pursuing the existence
To not care for you.

Often times I tell myself that this feels too good to be right.
Sometimes blinding myself of the possibilities that you just might
Love me, kiss me, hold me like I was of you,
For you, made to do those things only to you and then
The personalities of me hold a meeting and remember.

I am remembering those times my love for you fell on stony ground.
I am remembering those times when you chose her over

me
I am remembering those times when my soul ached for
you
I remember drowning in an ocean of tears
I remember surviving a bitter winter with three fish and
five loaves.

Constantly telling myself, constantly saying, that I can't
fall for you.
Constantly wooing and pursuing the existence to not
care for you.

I remember he said he will never hurt you.
I remember when he did.
I remember he made you dinner.
I remember later he went and made love to someone
else.
I remember we told him we loved him.
I remember he ran away.
I remember he came back.
But did he promise to stay?

I can't fall for you. I have to fight my love for you.

I remember he said he loved me.
Only to say he was confused.
I remember he kissed me ever so softly.
Yeah, my knees buckled on that one, too.
I remember I died a sweet death and had dreams of
tomorrow.
He looked into my eyes and heard my heartbeat.
He touched my hand and tasted my essence.
He spoke to me.
He showed me he loved me.

I am afraid.
He frightens me.
If I give him my love, will he become savage?
Will it consume him, later forcing him to hate me?

And we he?
So we hold a meeting.
To grasp things logically.

Constantly wooing and pursuing the existence to not
care for you.
Constantly telling myself.
Constantly saying,
That I can't fall for you.

Wed Dec 7 15:36:42 2005

Apple Pie

I am feeling pretty good right now. I live a
complicated life, but hey I am a complicated woman. I
wish to make no apologies for it. So there. Today,
today I think I died a little more inside. I made a call
yesterday out of complete frustration. I made a silly
comment that may have scared him away from me. I
think I want to apologize, but not because I am truly
sorry. I want to because I don't want him to run away.
Yes, he means more to me than sex, but I just want
that with him. I have experienced so many wonderful
things with him of course I want to share that, as well.
But who knows? I don't want him in my life just for
that. I know he loves me, and I do owe him more than
that. I owe him the truth. I need to love him without
saying a word. I need to be all those things the Good
Book says I should. But I have fears. I fear that he is
going to hurt me. I fear that he is going to use me. I
fear that one day I will wake up and he will be gone. I
fear that he will decide that his love for me has waxed
cold and leave me for another. I fear that I will have
children with him and later hate him for not being all I
want and need him to be. But alas, who lives in fear. I
would be stupid not to try.

I love Barbette. And I value her advice, but she is going through the same thing I am. She loves a fool that is off somewhere with another woman. I call him a fool because, to me, Barbette is Superwoman Incarnate and he had her all. I actually knew him first. The other guy has a live-in family. My girl, being who she is, respects herself and women in general too much to break up a home already unhappy, but when feelings get into it, things get sticky.

So here I am. Not love sick. Not love crazy. Just aware. Love wants me to understand something I guess. It is a little scary but here I am. I am feeling pretty good right now. I am going to suck up every moment of it. If love has my number, than serve me. Hear my case. Understand my pros and cons. Understand why I behave the way I do. Understand the questions that I have. Excuse my pistol. I don't want to kill you, just shoot off your pinky toe if you think you are going to hurt me again.

So now that you got me here let me tell you what I think I want. He needs to love me.
He has to love me like Christ loves the church. You know: unconditional, sacrificial, without merit.
He has to love God, to the point where he understands that He is all he really needs.
He has to touch me. I need to be spoken to without words.
He needs to challenge me, love me, rebuke me and console me.
He needs to spoil me when I least expect it and tell me no when I feel I deserve it.
He has to be able to laugh with me, cry with me, fart, and smoke trees with me.
He needs to be me, my mirror, my reflection.

I do like flowers.

I do like forget-me-nots.
And oh, don't forget about hot apple pie a la mode.

Wed Dec 7 12:30:33 2005

Confession

I am deciding a couple of things for my life. I first am choosing to breathe for just one second and fully release all those things that are holding me back. I refuse to go crazy wondering if I will ever find love. I have better things to do with my life than entertain doubt and insecurities. I forgot that I am beautiful. I forgot that I am a good person. There have been too many times when I have tried to define and validate myself through the eyes of someone else. I am concerned about the thoughts of my family. I think that if they were out of my business and the concerns of my love life, I wouldn't feel so pressured to be with someone. Half of my family is rooting for him, and the other half is rooting for him. I have to breath again.

All this time, I have been consumed with the issue of finding a companion. Maybe I should get a fish. I have to remember that I am worth more. And

150

yes, I too am a hypocrite. I settle for the first man who tells me I am worth something. All the time I try not to fall into the traps that consumed my mother, but here I am. Falling. I am currently chasing after a man that is well... confused, wants me but also his lifestyle and I am just wooed. Now if someone else were to tell me this story I would tell her to move on. Go find someone that is worth your time and finds you worthy of his (or hers). I hate that I have become so insecure. I hate that in every other aspect of my life (mostly) I am so secure and in charge. But now I feel weak. I feel delicate and I want someone to take care of me. But guess what? That person may never come. Or I might die because of worry. I may think it to death instead of changing my life. I always say, if I want something different, I have to be different. This does not mean changing who I am; just changing how I attract people. I need to respect myself a little better in order for people to respect me. So I need to make decrees. I pledge to myself that I am loved- not because some man said I was, but because God loved me enough to let me live. Because I have air in my lungs. Because I am beautiful inside and outside. Because He give me mercy and grace. I am loved. I love myself. I forgot I did. I love myself enough to know when I am being treated unfairly. I feel that it was unfair for him to dump me on Dec. 17, 2004 and still be in my life intimately. I feel that it is unfair for him to say he loves me yet do, say the most fucked up shit to me. I am still hurt by the way I accepted that shit he gave me. I hate that he only wants me when I don't care to love him anymore.

I feel that it is unfair for him to tell me all the things I want to hear. Now he may actually feel that way but he can't respond to his feelings. I translate this as "I am lonely and I need a guarantee of emotional love. I know that you enjoy sex. I know that you are looking for a man to be all those things that you dream of, but I can't be that right now. But I will get your hopes up to ensure that I have somebody when I need them. You know that this is new to me and I am sorry. When I don't need you, you will know. But you are in my life to be my break in-case-of-emergency girl. In case I don't find what I am looking for in a man or woman I will call you. When I get through fucking over your heart maybe you will be ripe enough to settle for less than what you believe in and just be my baby-mama. I really want you to take what I give you when I give it to you. I want you to be the mother of my children because you are the only woman I trust and also I know that you will put up with my crap. Because, like I said, your love has always been consistent." I hate that I could not see that before.

I love my mother very much, but I don't want to be like her when it comes to relationships. Some of my most horrible experiences with my mother have been over men. Don't get me wrong. I am not saying that I am going to be lesbian or anything, but I just want to evaluate this. I have blocked out large parts of my childhood because I am severely scarred. I remember getting beat by my stepfather with a studded belt and my mother only said to not tell my father. I remember getting beat with an extension cord because my male teacher thought I wasn't being Christian enough. And even now in my so-called adult existence, she lives with a man that is dangerous to her psyche and wonders why her children won't see her. I am supposed to be an educated individual. I am supposed to be smart enough to know when I am in danger. I feel like I am in danger. I need time to heal. I need time to endorse my own self worth. I wish I could get away for a while. I wish that I could do something that would give meaning to someone. I probably need to move, get a hobby. Find a class. You know, something that will distract me long enough to fight my addiction.

I am addicted to the concept of love. I am haunted by its imagery. Everywhere I go it seems that someone is getting married. Someone is hooking up. Someone is having a baby or someone is turning gay because they have given in. I see couple kissing and touching and loving each other and I become envious. I want to be happy but I am falling into a trap that has devoured many women, even the strongest of our breed. I cannot doubt myself. I am worth more than that. I understand why that prophet wrote, "Don't judge another man's servant". I have been judging myself. I don't belong to me, yet I have been comparing myself to others' profound notions of happiness. The time for that to end is now. I am a good person. I love God. I love myself. I am the determinant factor in my own happiness and so I must walk in it. And today. I confess that I will love myself first, no matter what. I pledge to myself that I am worth more than my expectations. Choosing to settle for anything less will be a life of mediocrity. I can't *be* more because I truly think that I don't deserve more. I apologized for the mishap with him. I am not a whore. I am not a bitch if I say no. And if anyone else thinks otherwise, fuck them. Fuck them in the ass dry. I am gold. I am a queen. I am the mother of the future and the creator of all things beautiful. Not because I am an arrogant ass, but because my father said so. I know that Abraham is dead in body, but he is not dead in spirit. And one day I will see him again, but I cannot keep using his death as an excuse to stay locked up in turmoil. He would be yelling at me right now if he saw how I was handling my life. He would say, write it down. Let your stories make you some money. He would say, "So what hair school didn't work out for you, try something else. If you like to dance, then do that. If you like to sing, then do that, but don't just sit on your ass waiting for someone to give it to you. You can do anything with what you have right now and you are only at the beginning of your life." He would say that a real man looks for a real woman. "Be all those things that you want him to be. Don't live your life angry because it will do you no good. If worrying could add one brick to your mansion in heaven, than do it, but since it don't, than don't." My God is good to me. I am on the right path. It will be hard, but anything worth its weight in gold will not be easy to obtain. All things work together for the good of them who love the Lord and who are called according to his purpose. My life is purposed. My tears are purposed. Abraham's death was purposed. I am with purpose. My childhood was purposed. My future is purposed. It is already written. I think I will make it. I think this winter is temporal. I will stop looking for Mr. Right. I will look for me. I will search behind crevices. I will swim to caves in oceans. I will fly to mountain peaks and dig the earth 180 degrees. I will find me and I will be heaven-sent.

Translucent,

Naked,

Present.

UNIVERSAL TRUTHS

I was thinking the other day.
Just to myself, you see.
How I can love you more,
More experientially?

So me,
Myself
And I
And I
Decided to take flight
Dimensionally.

First dimension: I need for us to go beyond
thought. I already think of
you.

Second dimension: I feel you more than my
tongue feels the nectar of an
orange.

Third dimension: Physically I am close to
experiencing our entire Chi.

Fourth dimension: We have already met through
time and space. I died at your
birth.

Fifth dimension: How do you explain the least
level of god-hood?

Infinity:	No need for numbers, just love.

12.31.2005

<u>F*** Slave</u>

The first thing I can do is laugh.
Laugh at you,
The man who asks for head like it is drinking water,
The man who prefers to jam it in your ass without anal
ease.
I laugh at you when you say,
I still treat you like a sex slave.

The man who fantasizes about me being Union Station.
The man that says, "its just sex."
I laugh at you when you say,
I still treat you like a sex slave.

The man who encouraged me.
Will I fuck my friend in front of you?
The man who thinks a compliment is,
"Oh, your titties so big."
Then grabs them like a lost retarded kid.
I laugh at you.

You hypocrite.

Stop asking me what I want if you are going to throw it
in my face.
To call me selfish.
Stop asking me questions you don't want answers to.
Don't ask me what I am thinking.
To then use it as an excuse not to
Touch me,
The way
I want

To be touched.

How do you understand fuck me hard?
Yet in all your sexual liberty,
Don't understand,
Touch me soft.

You are not a fuck slave.
You are a fucking hypocrite.
Bitch.

1.16.2006

Déjà Vu

You was with your best friend
Always whispering
About the state you want to be in.

I was just some big fool
Thinking it was cool
To give you all my love until then,

I found out
That you were not about
To share your heart and soul with me.

It was all a face
To just keep me in place
And experience all my grace.

So I'm standing here
Hoping it was just a dream
Trying hard to really see you,

But my future self
Is giving me some help
Déjà vu just said, "Don't love you."
Déjà vu just said, "Don't love you."

Déjà vu.

1.16.2006

Train Tracks

If you want to escape the pains of your soul?
Stop fantasizing about train tracks that lead to
nowhere.
Stop wondering how buildings fell on top of your
escape route.
These tracks in Chicago go to places now unseen.
But these roads all lead to the past.
A past that your soul is haunted by.
Acknowledge other possibilities that are now here.
Embrace this thing called the present.

March 29, 2006

Conversation

I am choosing to have a baby. I am currently dating
someone else. He does not want to have children
but I do. He and I have talked numerous times
about me having a child. Now that that time has
come, now that that decision is made. I have to
inform him of my plans now.

There is no experience that you are required to do.

I know that he loves me, but recently he has been
battling depression and I don't know if this is a

161

good thing to tell him now. I am scared that it might damage our chances for a future.

This concern really has nothing to do with his well-being. This has everything to do with your need to feel secure. If you are going to be concerned about his well being, then do that and love him. But if you are concerned with securing a nest egg for the future, address that. Don't use him as an excuse for your own fears.

But his actions recently have made me consider not having a future with him that is more than friendship. I want to have a child because I desire to. I would also desire a friend, lover and companion. All these things I found in him when he felt good about himself. I hold on to the fact that we tell each other the truth at all cost. This is because the relationship between friends is more important than anything. So, with that regard, I am going to tell him of my decision. The only issue now is when. I feel that the more I plan, the more I keep it from him, and I will hurt him more.

Seek ye first the kingdom of God and all these things will be added unto you. Keep me first. You will know when.

I have accepted that the possibility exists that he will hurt. I have accepted the possibility that he might have changed his mind about he and I conceiving. So I want to lay down all my fears regarding this beautiful choice that I have made so that I can handle it.

I don't have much money, as I would like to
finance this conception.

*Money is an illusion. If you fear not having money
that will come to you, brokenness. If you want
money, that is what will come to you, the want.
Instead, give it away. Understand that you have all
you need to do this. Those things you desire will
come if you simply give it to someone else. So
during your pregnancy, be kind and kindness will
come to you. Be love, and love will come to you.
Provide a since of peace and peace will provide for
you. Help others get fit and you will be fit. This is
because there is only one of us. That is the way of
the universe. That is the understanding of God. That
is the way in which you are created. Create this
child. Give gifts of money if you wish to see money.*

I don't know what the pain will be like.

*The pain will be as you choose it to be. You are a
thinking creature. Create your environment. You
don't have to be a victim to hormones, words or
actions. You feel these things because you want to
remember the experience. You wish to tell stories
that you have lived. You know its face.*

I don't know if I want to be married later.

*You will know when you choose to. Like you chose
to have this child. The child was made manifest
when you decided to have it. Even though you
cannot see her right now, he is right there waiting
to have that experience. You don't know if you want
to be married is a well thing. That means that you
are open to the experience, but limited in your*

perception of whom. The 'who' that you see now
may not be the who later. Planning shows maturity,
but it will not completely serve you to your
expectations if you confuse your true concerns with
the illusion of fear.

If I do decide to get married, will he still want me?

That would be predicting the future. Which is, of
course, ever-changing. Most times fear comes from
the obsession of knowing, or wanting to know the
others soul. That soul governing that body is that
soul's business. Instead remember that you don't
need anything seeing that your needs are already
met. Consistent entertaining of fears only brings
them into existence. Not saying don't be real and
feel these things, but feel them to experience them,
or not, choose and move on to the next grandest
thought.

How is this really going to impact our lives?

This will be your greatest experience yet.

How will my interaction with his family be?

Who cares? How will your interaction with his
family be? How will that interaction with your
family be? So many what if questions and not
enough peace. Quiet your soul and enjoy the ride.

Will they treat me different, because they really
don't know the extent of our relationship?

Let your words be given in love. Make your words
soft and stern. Remember who you are and then

remember who I am. Then remember that we are
one. This will guard your heart and mind. Think of
Christ.

I don't want to develop inappropriate feelings for
the other?

What you resist will persist. Be free. Be without
boundaries. You two will continue to evolve and
communicate with wisdoms. Not because you are
experts, but because you will be one in the raising
of this child. One foundation. One parent. You will
consider my wisdom as a basis and include me in
your oneness. Remember. Re-member.

I want to continuously respect his lifestyle choice.

Stop wanting and do. Stop hoping and be. If you
love him, you respect him.

I don't want to tell him until after he and I sleep
together.

Choose. Than continue to choose that same choice.
This is how the master of choice became masters.

I will not lie to him, but how can I say this truth in
love, with dignity and respect?

Talk to him as you would to me. Remember who I
am and you will remember who he is. Your
reverence for me will be laid at his feet. Your honor
for me will be in your words. Do this without fear
and expectations. That way it will be genuine. It will
be naked truth. Give him the dignity to choose.
Bless him with the freedom to choose. Then find, see

the perfection in his choice. Love me for it, love him
for it, and love yourself, for being love.

Maybe it is only best if I was just friends with him
as well. I will have a baby to take care of.

Forget the term "best." This is not a question but a
resolution. You will not replace one addiction with
another. End that here and continue to evolve in the
grandest version of you. You are more aware now.
You choose to forget that at times.

How will I deal with the pressures of life?

As you always have and you always will.

Hello There Sis,
When you get a chance, could
you print out the list for the
CRAZY PEOPLE doctors? I tried
to get the info from the Internet,
but I couldn't get through.

Thanks a bunch,
-Starr

First I just wanted to say SHUT UP. Dear, you are okay. If I thought you were taking me for granted, I would probably just beat you up. Any who, it is good to hear from you. I don't really know when the next rehearsal is but I'm sure someone, somewhere will call. Don't worry about any of it. You are a beautiful person who is also pretty hot. I just want you to know that. You can have all your hearts desires if you believe and know that you DON'T NEED THEM TO MAKE YOU HAPPY. Only you and God can do that. So, I leave you with this: be happy first, then you will truly be happy.

-T

<u>Size 14</u>

I took a good hard look at the mirror today.
I saw the woman that peered out at me.
I look and said out loud, that is the woman you grew up to be.
There she is, with full lips,
thick hips,
Baring the natural tone of her fingertips.
There she is

I took a good hard look at the mirror today.
I saw the curves of a goddess.
The markings of a priestess.
The wrinkles of a queen.
I read the stories of yester year from breast to breast.
I swam the road in between.

I saw her eyes
And how she cried, happy of course.

But remembering, remembering that course of jumping
through hoops.
Living a lie, barely living.
Singing gospel hymns to the basin of a toilet.
Beating Negro spirituals through the popping of pills.
Lying and testifying saying I don't want...
Just one more bite.

Just to see the pounds fade.
Watching my ass drop.
While tits just flop and flop from lack of fat.

The fact was that I didn't give a damn.
Who cared that I was six feet, so in theory
I could hold the extra meat.
Nothing left to do but push to be that size 2.

So I worked.
I studied.
I prayed.
I binged.
I sung.
I purged.
I hoped and dreamt that he would come and feed my ass.
Until the blood filled my mouth.
Choking the woman in the looking glass.

So I went to the gym.
The fork in the middle of the road became a participant
in juicy orgies of steak and potatoes.

No sad stories. To many of them already told, but
instead a haiku:

> Deddy transcended.
> But as far as I can tell.
> I still have to live.

No sad love songs.

Tony, Tamia, Brandy and even Floetry smoke flowing
trees with such sweet renditions of honey rum.
I didn't think I would need him.
So how did he become...

My tortured self looked back at me.
Through tears of relief.
Her being danced.
And proclaimed finally.
Just happy,
That I'm happy to be me.

With full lips
Thick hips
Baring the natural tone of my finger tips.

The opiate in my veins, I only wish to see the colors of your song.

<u>Revelation</u>

And my inner me.
Therefore, covered and filled me
With intensity.

I Got a Secret

I write for you.

The one who didn't fit in as a kid.
The one who was a leader whose only wish was to be held
So I tell you what your soul wants, needs to hear.
It will be alright.
You are loved by me and I appreciate you.
You can make it.
You are more than what your momma/daddy/sister/brother/that motherfucker said.
This too will pass.

I don't have time to defend my relationship with the Lord right now.
Because God knows me, cares, will and always will.
So if you are one of those people that are so holy ghost-minded, and no earthly good, get the fuck up off my square, because I am here to save lives.
The language is only going to get worse.

I am tired of telling people that they are going to Hell.
I would rather tell them how to live in Heaven.

I am tired of using biblical syntax to hide my psyche.
I would rather tell you how I feel.

I am tired of judging you.

171

I would rather kiss your cheek.

I am tired of you feeling uncomfortable around me.
I would rather you feel safe.
You know why?

Because I love Jesus.
So let me tell you about my Jesus.

My Jesus washed feet.
My Jesus fed folk.
My Jesus healed folk on the Sabbath.
Turned water into wine.
Beat folks with a whip for being out of line.
Knew when bastards were going to rat him out, and
still loved them.
And then died. Damn. Died.

So if you are one of those people that are so holy
ghost-minded, and no earthly good, get the fuck up
off my square, because I am here to save lives.
The language is only going to get worse.

I write for you.
That woman at the well.
That man that was dead.
That woman with the issue of blood.
That man possessed by devils.
That hoe.
That bitch.
The crack head.
That baby daddy.
That nappy-headed kid.
That fat girl.
That goofy boy.
That crazy person.

                              That fast ass little girl.
                           That coke slanging nigga.
I write for you.

I am tired of wearing sharp suits every Sunday just
to say, "Praise the Lord saints. Praise the Lord in
Jesus name."
I would rather get gritty with you in the field.

I am tired of looking at her swollen stomach and
naked ring finger.
I would rather rub her feet.

I am tired of hating on his boyfriend, when the
pastor is doing the same damn thing.
I would rather tell you to live.

I am tired of all the fucking so-called hypocrites.
If you saw Jesus today, you would probably put him
out the church.
He would probably stink from all the real work of
witnessing.
He would probably be dirty from travel and
touching those who are living on lower,

lower

Wacker.

    He would probably have a head full of locks. Who
       has time to be pretty when people are hurting?
                                              Crying.
           Shiting on themselves trying to beat heroin.
        Shaking their babies trying to keep them quiet.
                      Talking to all their personalities.

Holding the blade to her wrist because her momma
called her a dike.
Tooting before the board meeting.
Praying.
Praying for someone who would rather…

Tell them to live.
Rub their feet.
Get "crunk" with them in the city.
Whip folks for being out of line.
Turn water into wine.
Heal them on the Sabbath.
Heal them.
Make them feel safe.
Kiss their foreheads.
Tell them how you really feel.
Tell them how to live in Heaven.
In peace.
In quiet.
In love.

I would rather you try to see God.
I would rather you think about those questions that
make your skull scream.
Think about it… In the beginning God created the
earth. And the earth was without form, and void; and
darkness was upon the face of the deep. And the Spirit
of God moved.
Think about the beginning of the beginning.
Think about the Absolute of God.
The Master of the Un-movable, Movement.
Think about the existence of existence without
form.
And void.
Now think of you.
You say you know God.

Than you would know that there is only really one of us.
I'll prove it.

"As ye have done it unto one of the **least of these** my brethren, ye have done it unto **me**... In as much as ye did it not to one of the **least of these**, ye did it not to **me**.
(Matthew 25:40)"

Why would Jesus say that?

"Believe me that I am in the Father, and the Father in me: or else believe me for the very works' sake... the works that I do shall he do also; and greater works than these shall he do; because I go unto my Father.
(John 14:11-2)"

Think about the beginning of the beginning.
Think about the Absolute of God.
Now think of you.
You say you know God.
Than you would know that there is only really one of us.
Because God knows you, cares, will and always will.

It will be alright.
You are loved by me and I appreciate you.
You can make it.
You are more than what your momma/daddy/sister/brother/that motherfucker said.
Because you are here to save lives.

www.ingramcontent.com/pod-product-compliance
Lightning Source LLC
Chambersburg PA
CBHW031301090426
42742CB00007B/548